MASTERS AT WORK

BECOMING A SOMMELIER

BECOMING A CURATOR

BECOMING AN ARCHITECT

BECOMING A FASHION DESIGNER

BECOMING A SPORTS AGENT

BECOMING AN INTERIOR DESIGNER

BECOMING A FIREFIGHTER

BECOMING A NURSE

BECOMING A VIDEO GAME DESIGNER

BECOMING A MIDWIFE

BECOMING A TEACHER

MASTERS AT WORK

BECOMING A VIDEO GAME DESIGNER

DANIEL NOAH HALPERN

SIMON & SCHUSTER

New York   London   Toronto   Sydney   New Delhi

Simon & Schuster
1230 Avenue of the Americas
New York, NY 10020

First Simon & Schuster hardcover edition December 2020

SIMON & SCHUSTER and colophon are
registered trademarks of Simon & Schuster, Inc.

For information about special discounts for bulk purchases,
please contact Simon & Schuster Special Sales at 1-866-506-1949
or business@simonandschuster.com.

The Simon & Schuster Speakers Bureau can bring authors to
your live event. For more information or to book an event,
contact the Simon & Schuster Speakers Bureau at 1-866-248-3049
or visit our website at www.simonspeakers.com.

Manufactured in the United States of America

3   5   7   9   10   8   6   4   2

Library of Congress Cataloging-in-Publication Data

Names: Halpern, Daniel Noah, author.
Title: Becoming a video game designer / Daniel Noah Halpern.
Description: First Simon & Schuster hardcover edition. | New York :
Simon & Schuster, 2020. | Series: Masters at work |
Includes bibliographical references.
Identifiers: LCCN 2020032868 (print) | LCCN 2020032869 (ebook) | ISBN
9781982137939 (hardcover) | ISBN 9781982137946 (ebook)
Subjects: LCSH: Video game designers—Vocational guidance—
United States. | Video games—Design.
Classification: LCC GV1469.3 .H353 2020 (print) |
LCC GV1469.3 (ebook) | DDC 794.8/1535—dc23
LC record available at https://lccn.loc.gov/2020032868
LC ebook record available at https://lccn.loc.gov/2020032869

ISBN 978-1-9821-3793-9
ISBN 978-1-9821-3794-6 (ebook)

FOR CHRISTINA

TABLE OF CONTENTS

BECOMING A
VIDEO GAME DESIGNER

1

THE UNIVERSE,
ALSO KNOWN AS THE GAME

Here are three moments, from three universes:

First: the Unkillable Demon King has taken the form of Orianna, the Lady of Clockwork, for battle. He knows they've won when he traps Kuro for his partner's backdoor gank. It's all over once they kill Baron and wipe the other team out of the top lane. Afterward, he eats a chocolate bar. This is 2016, or no time at all.

Then: Poncho jacks in after picking up the contract. Once she's in the matrix, on the boat, she lowers the railing, deploys a launcher, launches herself to the airship. Three minutes through the door to do the job. At the elevator shaft she gets out the autocase, deck, and CCTV module, punches in "setpos 699-32-206" to aim the autocase, exits the aimbot, and enters the blink. The trunkline's in the Psychocortical Practice Room, whatever that is; she connects the phone to the deck, downloads it, scrams. It's only later, after she's jumped back to the Farfig, that she realizes she's forgotten to grab the autocase, left it behind. She's getting older, a little tired. This is 1980, or no time at all.

And finally: 14.Bxe7 Qb6 15.Bc4 Nxc3 16.Bc5 Rfe8+ 17.Kf1 Be6!! That was, almost indisputably, 1956.

You are forgiven if you do not know where you are. Only with time will a universe teach you to navigate inside its borders.

The first universe you are observing is the world of Runeterra. Runeterra is the setting for *League of Legends*, which, in what is often referred to as the real world, is a tremendously popular free-to-play video game. *League of Legends* requires you to choose a "champion" as your digital proxy and then team up with four other players in order to kill five opponents, as well as avoid or defeat other murderous obstacles, all within a fantasy realm of dragons and swords and magic fireballs. This particular instant is split in two, half taking place in Runeterra and half back here on earth: the moment of victory by this world's most famous professional *League of Legends* player, a young South Korean named Lee Sang-hyeok, also known as Faker, also known as the Unkillable Demon King, in the semifinals of the e-sports 2016 *League of Legends* World Championship.

The second universe begins in a place called Nuevos Aires and continues into a virtual reality within it. This is the video game *Quadrilateral Cowboy*, a cyberpunk hacking game that asks you to commit a series of heists on contract, using a computer you build to enter a matrix within the matrix—a digital world within its digital world. Your exploits begin on New Year's Eve as 1979 recedes and the '80s approach, somewhere within the early morning of cyberspace. You—as Poncho—get your assignment, case the job, log on with your portable deck and launcher and lantern, and enter the cyberspatial target. You have two friends and colleagues, Lou and Maisy; you have a square head and blue hair and a portable Vinylman to play your favorite records; you have three seconds to disarm the lasers and sneak in.

The third universe isn't a universe at all, really. It's chess. This is the moment a thirteen-year-old Bobby Fischer sacrificed his queen to his opponent, Donald Byrne, then one of the top-rated adult players in the country, a shocking and brilliant move that led Fischer to victory and to the beginning of his legend.

That is the experience of beginning to play a new game: What is this place? How does it work? What is the language they speak here? Gank, blink, check. Oh! He took my pawn!

Oh look, I can fly if I eat the green thing. Oh look, if I hit the space bar I jump up. Oh, see that, I—wait, how did I die?

The gods and minor divinities who make these universes have many names, but the ones who choose how the universe, also known as the game, will work are game designers. How does the rook move, can you launch yourself through space, and, wait, how do you stop? Do you remain invisible when you hide in the weeds, and can you try to jump out to kill another champion from behind? Game designers invent the things you can do in games, and they decide what you can't. They decide whether you can castle your king and rook just to the left, or both to the left and the right; whether you can pick up a vase and break the window of a doorless room you've been stuck in for too long. They create and adjust the rules of a universe you've chosen to enter. They decide if you can fly or not. They decide if you can talk to your friends or if you float around deaf and mute. They decide that you must murder an innocent little girl if you want the slug that lives inside her and which will give you great power to defeat your enemies. They decide that you cannot pass, that you cannot understand, that you cannot know, that you must die here, in this place. But they also decide that you can—you can understand, you can know. They make a door just for you and refuse to let you enter by it. They make a hole for you to jump through. They're the reason so many people come here to live. That is, to play.

It wasn't so long ago that most adult Americans considered video games nothing more than toys for children, time-wasters. Many still do, perhaps. Mindless, worthless, silly. Marginal to culture, or even entirely outside it. Corrosions to the social fabric. Incitements to carnage, instructions for nihilism. Violent delights with violent ends.

While the country was trying to decide whether video games represented something utterly unimportant or instead the utter and total destruction of society, something happened. Video games began to leave other entertainments behind. They started to make money—more money than books, music, or movies. They became the most popular and lucrative entertainment category in the country. They started to innovate—to use the form and technology of games to do things that other entertainment had never done before. They became something new.

Creating a video game requires a variety of skills, and so this growth, and this innovation, has a host of authors.

Founders, visionaries; programmers and artists and writers; marketers and salespeople and quality testers and so on. But the technology and the art, the storytelling and the coding, exist outside of games: in dishwashers and phones and thermostats, in museums and galleries, in books and television shows. What doesn't exist outside of games are games. That is: how the game works; what makes it a game. Above all, perhaps, what a new game needs are rules. Structures. Goals and objectives. How will it work? What are you trying to do when you play it? Where are you trying to go? What's stopping you? What's helping you? How do you navigate?

A video game designer answers these questions. A designer might choose whether you get two seconds or two minutes to complete a task. Or choose whether the rules of quantum mechanics apply in this new universe. Is there gravity here? Does gravity work the same way here as in our world? Should you have more teammates than enemies? Should you be able to detonate a nuclear weapon? Should you be able to run faster than the speed of sound? How do you win? How do you lose? Should you turn into a green walrus if you eat the red chickens? Should you be a good goose or a bad goose?

What would be more fun? This—or that? That—or this?

2

ACCUMULATING THE FACT

Tom Cadwell is head of design and R&D at Riot Games. Riot is responsible for *League of Legends*, which is to say responsible for a game—for ten years, the only one the company has made—that's free to download and play on your computer but pulls in around $2 billion a year. Cadwell is also senior vice president of the company, with certain executive and management responsibilities, which he seems good at, though it's being in the trenches, knocking around ideas about exactly how a game will work, that really lights him up. When I first met him he was thirty-nine, approaching forty: a large person, six foot three and 230 pounds (though on a fairly scientifically rigorous program to drop a bit of that weight), with short dark hair, pale skin, rectangular wire-rim glasses, and an extraordinary ability for creating systems that, translated through code and art and narrative and color and sound, come out on a screen as a game hundreds of millions of people might tell you, more than you really even want to hear it, is the coolest thing ever.

We met at Riot's Santa Monica headquarters, which sit on a nondescript stretch of Olympic Boulevard, not far from the Pacific Ocean. The entrance to its suite of buildings isn't imposing; it gives you no sense of how much it contains. In the foyer there are mounted screens displaying livestreams of the game itself, a few couches and tables. There are two twenty-foot-high black monoliths forming a narrow entrance to what lies within, and then, as you enter the place where the work is done, you're greeted by a gigantic bear with glowing eyes, surrounded by other life-size inhabitants of Runeterra. Even so, none of that quite prepares you for the maze-like expanse beyond, scores and scores and hundreds and hundreds of large black computer monitors, in rows, in gigantic open room after room, with airplane-hangar-height ceilings, each monitor manned by someone hard at work to make this one game just a little better—just a little more fun.

How do they figure out what that would be? That is, what are the fundamental ingredients of a good game designer? To begin with: someone who loves games. Someone who plays games. Someone who can't help but think about how games work. "I played thousands of games, or at least, close to a thousand, through my childhood," Cadwell told me. We were sitting in a conference room on the Riot LA campus. "It might not have been good for much else, but it was excellent training to be a game designer."

Cadwell is by nature a tinkerer, someone who likes to take things apart to understand how they work. The tinkering goes hand in glove with knowing: he is also by nature a knower. Someone who, if he's going to do some gardening, is going to do extensive research into best practices and new innovative thinking in gardening techniques; someone who is not just going to hire a money manager to look after the wealth the rapidly expanding video game industry can provide without studying financial markets himself. He wants to know. And then he's going to tinker some more.

"I just always want to understand how things work as systems," Cadwell said. "Accumulate the fact. Figure out the pattern."

Early on he fell in love with playing video games, and likewise early on he set about figuring out the patterns of video games, investigating their systems. Why was this one fun and that one not? He thought about that a lot. Wouldn't it be more fun if this one could do that, and that one could do this? Why was this one so easy? What made that one so hard?

Cadwell was born in St. Louis and grew up there, for the most part. His mother had been an elementary school teacher before he was born, and then stayed at home as well as doing some substitute teaching and nonprofit education administration. His father worked for a company that made silicon wafers. When Cadwell was seven, he got a Nintendo for Christmas; a computer came a year later. "I got a 286, which was lightning fast at the time," he said—this was the late '80s—"and I just explored it. On the Nintendo, *Super Mario Brothers* was the one I played the most, some other stuff—the Nintendo classics—but really, *Super Mario Brothers*, that and *Zelda*."

Cadwell speaks very fast, likes to pace when he's talking about something personal or complex, has a face that gives a notion of what he looked like when he was seven. It's not just that he spends his days thinking about games that provide a window into something boyish; it's not just that he wears T-shirts and cargo shorts to work, either, or that he works in an industry that has long been portrayed as a thing for children. It has to do with his grin, his body language, his energy when he gets onto topics that interest him. The excitement, the thrill of building something in the world that he's imagined in his head, is a particular type of joy not expressed much in adulthood. It has to do with the way he aims his focus on what he wants to explain, a childlike focus, in the best sense—pure and clear, like there is an object that exists in perfect abstraction in his brain and thus requires precision to be transformed from its blueprints into language. The way he sometimes closes his eyes to picture the concept he wants to describe. The way he grins only just slightly and, occasionally, flicks his eyes at you just for an instant to check if you're with him, that you understand why the thing you and he are talking about is so great.

After Cadwell finished sixth grade, his father transferred to Seoul to build and operate a new plant in South Korea, bringing along the family of four—Tom has a younger sister—for a year. Cadwell had had some difficulty with the social aspects of school—he preferred reading and playing games on his own—but Korea opened him up, gave him a broader perspective. "I definitely had trouble relating to people growing up, and now I don't as much," he said, "and I think Korea helped me be more flexible and just gave me some understanding that we're all different in our own ways. But games were always a refuge I could go to, and a place I could grow, or at least in some of them. Mostly I would just play the games intensely myself, and honestly I was kind of antisocial, and I think perhaps that I did reduce my social development, but I was left with a really deep understanding of why this game is fun and why this game is not fun and why I stick to this game and bounce from that game."

When Cadwell returned to the U.S., in 1993, he had an easier time finding friends. And he found kids who shared his interests. "I'd hang out with the geeks and nerds crowd, as you might expect, given my profession, but also with kids who weren't," he told me. Not only that, but a revolution had quietly taken form and swelled up and come to St. Louis: Cadwell was now connected to the internet, which transformed the experience of games. Before, to play, say, Dungeons & Dragons, you needed not only your twenty-sided die and your Dungeon Master's Guide but also live people who wanted to play and could get their parents to give them a ride to your house. Online, they were easier to find. This was the first age of dial-up, and Cadwell entered it eagerly.

Cadwell went deep into multiplayer real-time virtual world games, known as MUDs ("multi-user dungeons"). His first loves in the incipient world of internet MMOs (massively multiplayer online games, with very large numbers of players) were *Toril* and then *Duris*. (These were player versus environment, and then player versus player, combat-Dungeons-and-Dragons kinds of games.) He also liked finding communities that were inventing better and better ways to play the games: for instance, someone might invent a "macro," or a shorthand command, that would allow players to almost instantly have their desires manifest on-screen instead of typing out an entire extensive command. (Much of video game hacking has to do with doing everything faster.) It makes sense that people building their own interfaces appealed to him. In general, he liked doing things his own way, opening up the bodies of games and dissecting and rearranging the constituent parts. He wasn't a hacker, per se. "I messed around a little, but didn't get too seriously in it," he said, and entirely avoided the sort of black hat behavior the movies would start portraying, like phone fraud or breaking into servers. Still, he didn't always follow the rules. The administrators of *Toril* kicked him off their servers for being too materialistic while playing a paladin, meant to be chivalrous and heroic; they flipped his class to a fighter, which, Cadwell said, "was unusable for the stats I had, so I was like, okay, cool. I guess I'm done." He might have been done with *Toril*, but that just meant there would be a new game on the horizon.

Cadwell entered MIT in 1997, planning a science major of some kind, interested in chemistry, or maybe engineering, though he eventually chose to concentrate in computer science. He also discovered a new game: *StarCraft*. *StarCraft* had come out in March 1998, a real-time strategy (RTS) space-opera game that takes place at the other end of the galaxy (in the Koprulu Sector). The action commences in the twenty-fifth century; there are three species battling it out in space. The Terrans (humans), the Zerg (insects), and the Protoss (space elves with advanced technology) fight for dominance, with the player choosing one of the species to lead, directing a military campaign. The humans want to survive, the elves want to protect their world, and the insects just want to kill everybody. Fast reflexes help, but above all it's a strategy game, now considered a classic of the genre.

"I was pretty terrible, and then I was pretty good," Cadwell said. Pretty good: he was one of the best *StarCraft* players in the world. He maintained a blog on strategy, writing about mineral resources and land testing and deriving force equations. "So I was regarded as someone who understood a lot about the game and was, you know, pro-ish," he told me. That went on for a while, until he realized the triumphs of the Koprulu Sector had hidden costs. "I quit playing after the beta," Cadwell said, "because I was failing out of MIT."

He was playing the game seventy hours a week. He wasn't going to class. He wasn't seeing friends. "You know, um, it reached an unhealthy level for me," he said. (Cadwell likes to deploy understatement, sometimes to check if you're paying attention, and sometimes just because he's generally understated.) And he realized he did not want to move to a training commune and practice eighteen hours a day to be a pro gamer. He just wasn't going to do that. Instead, he started going to class. And went out and saw some friends. But he also sat down and wrote out a design doc. That is, he sat down and wrote down an idea for a game.

"It was terrible," Cadwell said. But it was a beginning.

The game would be *Strifeshadow*, another RTS game, and did not turn out to be quite as terrible as he describes the original plan to have been. He'd written up his design doc based on a template he found on the internet—something, he says, that he would not recommend today. "I think it's much more important to clearly articulate what you're trying to achieve and then go through the technical details as you're building them, because the context is so important.

Design documents were from an era when games were built to spec, and the cost-control efficiency was really important in there. There was some iteration there"—loosely, design by trial and error, a cumulative process—"but it was more like, 'We know what we're doing, we're just going to build it.'" Instead, he prefers a collaborative approach in which you document what you're doing as you do it. Let the process lead you.

It would take two and a half more years for the game to get built. In the meantime, he had righted the academic ship and was approaching graduation with a degree in computer science. He'd done a summer internship at the game company Pandemic Studios after his sophomore year, and designed "a crappy web game," a "get-elected simulator," for his senior thesis. He doesn't remember what it was called. "I was trying to create a cynical web simulation of running for political office. Hush money. Oh no, skeletons in your closet! Too ambitious. I didn't have the technical ability to execute it, or the design ability."

But the original RTS design he'd made had attracted some interest when he shopped it around, and so, still a student, he was recruited by a young game company founder, Martin Snyder, who was looking for his own RTS game.

It was too good an opportunity to pass up, so, while still at MIT, Cadwell began working thirty to forty hours a week as a designer for Snyder's operation, making *Strifeshadow*.

Upon graduation, though, he felt he wanted safe, secure work. "I think I accepted the pragmatic wisdom of adults in my life," he said, "which was that game development is kind of a crazy industry. It's less crazy now than it was then, but even today, nobody knows, and certainly nobody knew then, whether it was really a viable path." So he took a software job writing tools to allow portfolio managers to do something or other with mutual funds that had something to do with separate account products that I couldn't really follow. It didn't sound fun at all.

"Those guys were great. I really enjoyed working with them," Cadwell said. "But I was a programmer there, and, actually, they found me to be mediocre at programming, but really good at design, which is what I had been practicing."

Meanwhile, *Strifeshadow* had come out in 2001, with Cadwell credited as lead designer. It was a 2–D, multiplayer strategy game with, again, three species—the accursed, the sylvans, and the dark elves—and three different playing styles: undead, tricky, and furtive. It was long on complex, tactical decision-making and short on graphics. It also included a feature called StrifeEdit, which offered players the same tools the developers used to create the game, allowing them to create their own scenarios and maps and so on.

It did not set the world on fire. It sold around one thousand copies, according to Cadwell's memory. But he'd realized that game design was still calling to him. So he shopped his résumé around. It wasn't as easy to find something as he hoped—the industry and the practice of video game design were still so new that companies often didn't know what they wanted, or imagined they wanted only the very specific skills applicable to their specific games. Eventually he landed a job at Blizzard Entertainment, working on a game called *Warcraft III*, and its subsequent expansion.

Blizzard, based in Irvine, California, was the company responsible for *StarCraft*, but even bigger things were in the offing. *Warcraft III* was another real-time strategy game, with orcs and heroes and the like—the Burning Legion, the Scourge, the Horde—that was released in 2002, with an expansion pack a year later. It would be a predecessor to the phenomenon of *World of Warcraft*, the hugely popular massively multiplayer game, which was an internal company alpha at Blizzard at the time and which would go on to be played by hundreds of millions of people, making over $10 billion over the next fifteen years. *Warcraft III* was no dud either—it would sell around four million units. Cadwell had entered the big business of the burgeoning gaming industry.

Cadwell was hired as the lead play-balance designer. "When people think of play balance, usually they're talking about making the pieces of the game fair. Between sides, but it could be also between pieces—like this character is too strong, or it's unfair when you play that character. In soccer, say, you might be deciding how far outside the goal can the goalie hold the ball, for instance." A soccer design allowing the goalie to run all the way down the entire field to the other side's goal with the ball in his hands, for instance, and then to just stuff it in the opponent's net, might be an example of bad play balance. "Then again, there's a second order of play balance, which is: Which experiences are you cultivating, which experiences are you suppressing?"

For five or six months Cadwell worked seventy-five to eighty hours a week, what he describes as a fairly typical crunch, and then began gearing up for work on *World of Warcraft*. "I basically would just sit there and make massive lists of detailed game-design taste calls. Sometimes it was just bugs, like: 'This is misplaced in the world.' But also it would be something like: the way in which these monsters are placed causes a level of threat that's out of proportion with the intention of the area; or the monsters in these areas don't have any variation; or this item was not satisfying and it should be satisfying because of how hard I worked for it."

This was Cadwell's first experience working with a large team, and he had to learn how to navigate the social aspects of teamwork. It was satisfying work, and he was learning, but the video game industry at that time was not the high-paying world it would become. He worked under two people—Allen Adham and Rob Pardo—he admired and learned from, but he didn't see the upward trajectory he wanted. So he left LA for Chicago, for the Kellogg School of Management at Northwestern. Business school gave him a broader view on different career paths, and he decided the time had now come in earnest to move forward into a new chapter of adulthood. As he finished up, he intended to leave games behind. Predictably, perhaps, games weren't ready to leave him.

"I was interviewing at Bain Consulting, the LA office," he said, "and I was in the second round of interviews. They didn't offer me the job, which was disappointing. But I had gotten to the round with the partners, and they were nice guys, and they did say, 'We like your critical thinking skills, your independence of thought. You probably would be pretty good at this job. However, your passion is clearly for the game industry, and you should talk to Brandon Beck, who recently resigned'—he was an analyst or an associate—'who we really think highly of, and he's starting a game company and you guys might really hit it off.'"

Brandon Beck was a USC business school graduate who, with his friend and classmate Marc Merrill, had gone a more usual route at the time: from B school to Bain for Beck, and from B school to the U.S. Bank for Merrill. But they both loved video games—*StarCraft* and *Warcraft* among them—and eventually moved back to LA and set about creating their own company, just as Cadwell was looking for a new job. That company would be called Riot Games.

"So I met them," Cadwell said, "and I was like, 'Wow, these guys have no idea what they're doing. But they're really smart and their idea's pretty good.'"

3

A SCATTERED DYNASTY
OF RECLUSES

Once upon a time there was an early hominid. And possibly, at some point, this Early Hominid threw a rock at a mastodon he was hunting, or at a saber-tooth tiger, or at another Early Hominid, and missed; instead the rock hit a hollow tree, and it made a funny sound. "Ha, ha!" said Early Hominid, forgetting about the mastodon. And so he picked up another rock and threw it at the tree. This time he missed. And he tried again, and again, until he was out of rocks.

Maybe he had a friend. Maybe he said to his friend, "Hey, man, try to hit that tree with this rock. No, no, you have to throw it. Like this." Maybe he said, "I bet I can hit it more times than you." And maybe he said, "No, no, that's too close, you have to stand over here, behind the sloth bones, that's the rule. If you step over the bones it doesn't count."

Maybe the friend said, "Hey, how about if I hit it more times than you, I get the good part of your sloth meat."

"No, no," said the first one. "Just throw it."

That was a game.

A few hundred thousand years later or so, a physicist named William Higinbotham made another one. Higinbotham, who had worked as a member on the Manhattan Project in Los Alamos and later became a leading advocate against nuclear weapons, was working at the Brookhaven National Laboratory on Long Island in 1958 when he designed something for the lab's annual open house just for fun. With an analog computer, an oscilloscope, and electromagnetic relays (essentially, switches) he created what many game historians consider to be the first video game. It was called *Tennis for Two*, and it consisted of a small green blip (the ball) on a five-inch screen that you hit back and forth using a knob and a button. It was the hit of the open house. He didn't bother to patent it, and never made another.

That same year, a twenty-one-year-old man named Steve Russell was beginning work with John McCarthy and Marvin Minsky at MIT's new artificial intelligence lab. Russell joined an MIT group called the Tech Model Railroad Club, which had been founded in the '40s by a group of students who were interested in the workings of the automated operation of model trains, but would now rapidly become a workshop for the world's first hackers. The Signals and Power Subcommittee, who created the circuits that made the trains run, is credited with popularizing the term "hack," and establishing many of the ethical principles of hacker culture. Their dictionary of new terms, for instance, is often credited with authorship of the rallying cry "Information wants to be free."

In 1962, using the lab's new $120,000 PDP-1 computer (an upgrade from the three-million-dollar TX-0 they had been using before), Russell, in collaboration with his colleagues Martin Graetz and Wayne Wiitanen, made a game. They called it *Spacewar!* The game was a battle between two spaceships, maneuvering in the gravity well of a star. Both ships are controlled by human players. When it was complete, Russell left it in the lab for anyone to play—or to improve. *Spacewar!* became not only one of the first video games but also the first game with mods—that is, player-made modifications. One colleague from the lab hacked the game to encode the night sky, making the stars and constellations' placement and brightness more accurate; another added a sun with a gravitational pull. A third added hyperspace, giving players the ability to escape into a fourth dimension and reappear in another part of the game. Russell added a scoring system. The game was the first video game to be played at multiple computer installations. It tore through the small programming community of the '60s.

Russell's game, and others like it, were still the province of academics and researchers; it required access to a $120,000 computer to play *Spacewar!* Which is to say, this new thing—the video game, such as it was—was not really available to the masses to play. A young University of Utah graduate named Nolan Bushnell gets the lion's share of responsibility for changing that.

At the time, the University of Utah, along with Stanford and MIT, was one of the three top schools for the new field of computer science, and also one of the few to purchase a PDP-1. Bushnell found *Spacewar!* in the computer lab and became addicted. Up to this point, these games had been created to show what computers could do, or as experiments, or just for fun. Bushnell was interested in a fourth option. An entrepreneur by nature, he had worked the midway at a local amusement park near Salt Lake City, and he thought immediately of how much money a game like this could make at the right venue. That thought, a few steps down the road, would turn into the birth of the video game industry.

Almost a decade after Russell first finished *Spacewar!*, the technology to create that industry had just about arrived. Now living in Northern California, Bushnell had programmed a game called *Computer Space*, a knockoff of *Spacewar!* (And so began the proud tradition in video game design of taking a beloved game and changing it slightly to make a new game.) He designed it for a four-thousand-dollar Data General computer, but he realized that playing a computer game on a computer wasn't going to work when his initial efforts to market *Computer Space* flopped. So he built a circuit board meant solely for playing *Computer Space*, hooked it up to a TV he bought at Goodwill, and put the whole thing in a Plexiglas case, attached to a can for collecting quarters. A local arcade company contracted to produce fifteen hundred coin-operated *Computer Space* arcade games and distribute them on their pinball route, and with that, Bushnell had invented a new industry. Still, the game flopped again. This time, Bushnell decided to start his own company, with a partner, an engineer named Ted Dabney. They wanted to call the company Syzygy, but the name was taken, so they went with their backup, from the Japanese word used in the game Go that means more or less the same as "check" in chess: Atari.

By then, the inventor and former defense contractor Ralph Baer had created an interactive TV console for Magnavox with video table tennis—the first home game contained all in one package—and Bushnell wanted to do the same. He had decided *Computer Space* was dead, a bust; instead, the first product of Bushnell's company would be *Pong*, a simple game designed by an engineer he hired named Al Alcorn, in which two players used electronic paddles to send a blip back and forth across a screen—a moving picture to complete the feedback loop between the eyes, the brain, and the fingers. That was 1972. *Pong* was no bust. Bushnell had finally hit his moment. By 1974, Atari was making four million dollars a year in revenue.

The rest of the decade and the beginning of the '80s saw the widening gyre of what have come to be thought of as the classic arcade games: *Space Invaders, Galaxian, Pac-Man, Asteroids, Centipede, Missile Command*. Following Baer, Bushnell had also begun the momentous mass transfer of the video game from the arcade to the home, a concept that connected with the public, to say the least: home *Pong* was released for Christmas 1975, and in 1976, at least seventy-five other companies tried marketing home video game machines. Bushnell had a new idea to bring to market: the Atari 2600, a multi-game console with a joystick. Atari's revenues stood at $2 billion by 1980. By then, Bushnell was out—he'd go on to invent Chuck E. Cheese, and dozens of other companies—but the first golden age of the video game industry had arrived.

The next age, in some sense, was the age of Shigeru. Shigeru Miyamoto, the Japanese designer of *Donkey Kong*, *Super Mario Bros.*, *The Legend of Zelda*, and many more to follow: the most influential video game designer in the history of the practice. Miyamoto grew up in a small village in western Japan, a dreamy kid who liked reading and drawing, making puppet shows, and exploring the countryside. He studied industrial design in Kyoto, and, in 1976, after graduating, he arranged an interview through a family connection with Hiroshi Yamauchi, the president of the Nintendo company. Nintendo had been founded in 1889 by Yamauchi's great-grandfather. Its original business was playing cards made from mulberry bark. Now Yamauchi had built it into a powerhouse toy company and, having been watching the success of video games closely, had begun making his move into the space. Miyamoto brought wooden toys he'd made to the interview. He began working at Nintendo in 1977, hired as a staff artist. Shortly thereafter, he invented the modern video game.

He began by playing the games that had come before, investigating what made them fun. Miyamoto believed that video games hadn't borrowed enough from other forms, particularly film: they needed more drawn-out characters, better art. He thought, even more ambitiously, that instead of just warmed-over science fiction space opera and the like, they could draw from Shakespeare and the Bible. He felt they relied too much on anger and fear—making players mad at themselves for failing, making them kill, kill, kill, or be killed—and there was another world of childlike joy and pleasure to be plumbed.

For his first game, Miyamoto invented three characters, originally based on the cast of Popeye (Popeye, Bluto, Olive Oyl). They were called Jumpman, a portly carpenter; Donkey Kong, a stubborn gorilla; and the Lady they both love (unnamed). These choices—no aliens, no saving the universe—were just the beginning. The way the game was played was new as well. Giving Jumpman the ability to jump over gaps and obstacles was utterly innovative, and this style—which Miyamoto called a running/jumping/

climbing game—would come to be known as a platform game, and dominate the industry for years. Perhaps above all, the point was not simply just to accrue the most points, but rather to complete the story. Miyamoto had introduced a new level of narrative to video games. Earlier games had mostly been: aliens invade, you defend Earth from them. Or something similar. *Donkey Kong* gave the player at least the first gesture toward motivations, characters, story arcs.

But it was a sequel—*Super Mario Bros.*, in 1985—that saved and transformed the industry. In the early '80s the market for home games had crashed—too many shabby games flooding the stores—and many companies had gone under. Atari was bankrupt. The media had begun to treat video games like a fad whose time had come and gone. *Super Mario* came to the rescue. The game's point, again, was the rescue of a lady, this time kidnapped by an evil turtle. Jumpman had been renamed Mario and made a career change (he was now a plumber). Joined by a brother named Luigi, he bounces through the Mushroom Kingdom, dodging or bonking enemies and turning up helpful treasures, like magic mushrooms and gold coins. There are eight worlds, each with four levels: thirty-two stages to get to the princess. The game's mechanisms are uncomplicated, but the way they interact and play out gave players a sense of freedom, that the combinations didn't bump up against the glass. The restrictions of the game didn't continually remind you that you were outside the game, jamming the button frantically, but instead opened up a world to enter. The permutations felt more like chess than *Space Invaders*. It took Japan by storm first. By 1990, the game was in one in four American households, and *Super Mario Bros.* and its sequels had sold seventy million units. Polls showed that more American children knew Mario than Mickey Mouse. Miyamoto had renovated what had started to seem to the public like a hoary, used-up house. He extended this even further in *The Legend of Zelda*, a nonlinear game, a new world (or an old one—its universe is based on his childhood memories) with no apparent end.

A world with no end! That would be quite a trick of programming. At the very least, game developers began to reach out into new and different sorts of universes, each rapidly expanding. The next decade saw several major developments in design trends. First-person shooters like *Wolfenstein 3–D*, *Doom*, and *Quake* transformed the perspective of games: you were within the world, not monitoring the action from above or beyond. Similarly, puzzle games, like *Myst*, put you in first-person perspective, but instead of shooting things you explored and solved problems. And then there were the God games, which gave players the ability to create, control, and direct a universe themselves. In 1989, Will Wright created *SimCity* (the player designs and oversees a modern city), following it up with *SimEarth* (the same, for a planet), *SimAnt* (an ant colony), *SimLife* (an ecosystem), and eventually the blockbuster game *The Sims*, in 2000 (a family in an ordinary suburban environment). "It occurred to me that most books and movies tend to be about realistic situations," Wright has said. "Why shouldn't games be?"

These kind of open world, sandbox games—so named for their resemblance to a giant sandbox to play in, undirected, free, generally nonlinear, and without, necessarily, an end point—had antecedents as far back as the '80s but now began a new revolution. It was a new romantic notion ("Give them a sandbox, and they will build castles") that placed more power and control and responsibility in the players' hands. The games expanded the possible universes of games: they both allowed for explorations beyond limited permutations within levels, making the game a great circle rather than an arrow, as well as taking the public's attention further from aliens and dragons and closer to recognizable characters and landscapes. *The Sims* certainly did that, and the following year, *Grand Theft Auto III* (2001) extended the new canon as well. The massive success of *GTA III*, which put you in a 3–D world of crime and sex with a seemingly endless assortment of minigames and side missions, transformed the industry and the way the wider public looked at video games. These games were made possible by technological advances, particularly with what computer science could now do with automated systems and AI programs that elaborated nonplayer characters' behavior. These new horizons provided a new kind of broad experience. The universes they offered seemed boundless.

The next great transformation to sweep the popular imagination was the world of massively multiplayer roleplayer games (MMORPGs), notably *World of Warcraft*. The roots of these kinds of games returned to Dungeons & Dragons, the role-playing dice game, and to a few video games in the '70s and '80s. *World of Warcraft*'s own original ancestor, *Warcraft: Orcs and Humans*, came out in 1994. But *World of Warcraft*, which came ten years later, in 2004, was a quest game in a fantasy world that married a galaxy of interacting players with real-time strategy like no other before it. The return to the fantasy world of swords and spells was an overlay for a new kind of engagement: in an MMORPG, the player becomes a character, creates that character's identity, and becomes him or her, all the while interacting with a host of other player-characters, acting within the game's persistent world, which continues to exist and evolve even while the player is offline and away from the game. As thousands of MMORPG players turned to millions, and those millions upon millions spent hours and days and years inside the games, the MMORPGS began to develop their own subcultures, their own slang and language, their own economies—their own societies.

Meanwhile, games had moved from the arcade to the living room and now back out into the world, in the form of mobile gaming. Basic handheld games dated back at least to the '70s—electronic football, auto-racing, and the like. But beginning in the late '90s, the advent of the mobile phone gave rise to a new iteration of mobile gaming, and the sector was fully reinvented in 2008, with the introduction of Apple's App Store. While these early games were popular— *Snake*, a 1997 game preinstalled on Nokia phones, is estimated to have been on 350 million phones, and perhaps above all, *Tetris*, which had been invented in Russia in 1984, came to the iPod in 2006, and by 2010 had been downloaded more than 100 million times—the perception of them was as something marginal to the gaming world. The rapid spread of smartphones changed that. Fun, casual games like *Angry Birds* or *Candy Crush*—that is, easy to learn, without requiring great labors to achieve some level of mastery—changed how the public and the media saw mobile games and expanded the audience massively. Total revenue in 2008 for mobile games was $5.8 billion; less than a decade later, in 2017, mobile games made $50 billion, almost half of total video game revenue at the time.

The range of games continues to expand, as does the reach. Action games—platform games, fighting games, shooter games, and battle royale games—still dominate the market, accounting for almost half of all sales, followed by role-playing games and sports games. The free-to-play online (and console) game *Fortnite*, released by Epic Games in 2017, was made up of two modes initially: *Fortnite: Save the World*, a shooter-survival player-versus-environment game in which you shoot zombies and defend fortifications, and *Fortnite: Battle Royale*, a player-versus-player iteration in which as many as one hundred players compete to be the last avatar standing. (The following year, Epic put out *Fort-*

nite: Creative, a sandbox game mode, similar to *Minecraft*, with players able to create anything they want on an island, such as battle arenas, race courses, platforming challenges, and more.) In less than a year, *Fortnite: Battle Royale* had 125 million players, sprouting again new economies and virtual societies.

About 100 million people watch the Super Bowl. There are about 2.1 billion Christians in the world. Facebook has 2.45 billion users. And then there are 2.5 billion gamers. In 2019, the total global box office revenue—all the money movies made at the theater—reached about $42 billion, a new record for films. Video game consumers spent about $150 billion in 2019.

4

THE INFINITE HILL

League of Legends is what is known as a multiplayer on-line battle arena (MOBA) game. The player chooses one of around 150 available champions to play, makes strategic choices about what magic items or weapons to outfit him or her with, and is automatically teamed up with four players of more or less similar skill, whereupon they usually sally forth on a plateau called Summoner's Rift and battle five opposing champions, as well as opposing bots, called "minions." You might be playing with (or against) friends or strangers, teenagers from Topeka and accountants from Austin, a kid from Seoul, from Beijing, from Canberra.

Along the way there are computer-generated dangers aside from your opponents, including jungle monsters, dragons, and a gigantic purple spider-snake called the Baron Nashor who can spit acid. The game ends (usually it takes about thirty minutes) when one team destroys the other's Nexus, which is to say their home base.

The champions, which are categorized as assassins, marksmen, mages, and the like, vary widely. Some are easy to play and some complex; they have different offensive and defensive capabilities, but as they gain experience they become more powerful. Each player has a positional role on the map, called Top Lane, Jungle, Middle Lane, Bottom Lane, and Support. As you kill minions and opponents, you gain gold, which can be used to buy stuff to help you kill more opponents and get more gold.

It's a little confusing for people who haven't spent time in this kind of universe. You have been slain! New players may hear that one a lot. Figuring out how to outfit your champion—weapons, potions, and so on—can be an intense tactical computation for experienced players, and utterly baffling to new ones. Most new players stick to practice games—tutorials—and single-player games against bots until they know what they're doing.

League of Legends has a lineage that goes back to *StarCraft*, but its more recent genealogy comes out of a game called *Defense of the Ancients* (usually called *DOTA*), which in turn was a community-created mod of *Warcraft III*. To someone not terribly sophisticated about games—me—the two seem very similar on the surface. They look almost the same. That is to say, if you were to describe it as ungenerously as possible, one of the most popular games in the world appears at first untutored glance as basically a rip-off of a piece of fan fiction of another game. But going that far is more than ungenerous—it's unfair and inaccurate, because that's not the way things work in video games.

How the game looks is very different from how the game works. The proof is not in who made the newest new thing utterly unlike anything else that came before it: it's in who made the game people love the most. There's a reason many of the most popular games build off the ideas of their predecessors: a design that offers players something new in terms of how the game works tends to resonate in the industry more than inventing a new look, or a new story, or even a new genre. The way the new builds on the old ones echoes the way games are made—by iteration. Building and building, changing and changing, grand new floors on a continuing edifice reaching higher and higher, architectural styles and concepts developing and evolving as the game grows, until the top of the building—though it may stand on an original foundation—has become something entirely different from its base.

Narrative or aesthetic originality doesn't necessarily hold the same value in the gaming world as it has in the past in other forms of art and entertainment; originality of story and art are probably secondary to how the game works, what its rules and mechanisms are. What's more, the contribution that consumers of these products (or art objects, or works of entertainment) make to the products themselves—the way those consumers can affect the evolving form, function, and development of the game—is of an entirely different quality from those other forms of art and entertainment. The role of the player in games is not just that he or she interacts within the narrative by choosing to go left or right, but can transform the frame entirely, not acting within a context but instead creating a new context. That is a role that is of an entirely different order.

Cadwell began advising Riot's founders, Merrill and Beck, in 2006, though he didn't come on as a full-time member of the team until 2008. In the meantime, he worked at Red 5 Studios, founded by a group of *Warcraft* alums, and moved into the production side. He thought he was interested in moving away from design—but he couldn't resist it, and eventually returned to Riot, and back to design.

"Marc and Brandon laid out a bunch of product strategy

choices, especially outside the game, that I think were really important to its success," he said. "Free to play as a service, and picking the genre. Being oriented to an international audience instead of just the U.S. audience." Cadwell joined Riot full-time as design director, focusing on gameplay. His first order of business was clearing out stuff that he felt just wasn't working.

"In a single-player game," he said, "you make decisions in context of the player. How does the player feel, how does the player feel, how does the player feel. In a multiplayer game, you are interacting with other humans, who are also having experiences. And that makes it a different animal." A designer needs to ask how any decision affects all players in the game, not just the player who will be immediately affected by that decision. Each decision radiates out exponentially. "There's a bunch of stuff in *DOTA*, which *League of Legends* was inspired by, that I felt were poor design choices that tended to be fun for one player at an expense to other players. So whatever enjoyment that player was having, other players were having a far more negative experience, which meant the overall expense for the game was negative."

The team at Riot agreed that there should be a large

number of champions for players to choose from, that teams should be made up of five players (they also considered four or six). They decided that each of the players should have a different job (the position they play on the team, so to speak). "I think we had a meta one time," Cadwell said (meaning a "metagame," where you play the game to find the best and quickest means to victory), "where everybody would just go to the midlane, so we had to fix that: it wasn't fun gameplay." (That is, everyone wanted to play the same position.) "It was a design choice we made. Hey, there's less flexibility, but it's a more consistent experience, and then the complexity of game lies underneath that and not in that choice."

They did alpha testing with family and friends in early 2009, and beta testing in the spring through the summer. The game was released at the end of October. Cadwell remembers saying to Brandon Beck, "Yeah, I just don't know. How well do we need to do for this to be a going concern?"

Beck laughed at the finance term—a going concern—and said, "We get twenty- or thirty-thousand peak active users, we should have enough income that we can keep trying."

"What happens if we get five- or ten-thousand?" Cadwell asked.

"We'll be looking for other jobs," Beck said.

They did not get five- or ten-thousand. They did not get other jobs. They got 100,000 in two months. The free-to-play model on the PC was still new, and although the popularity of the model would spread worldwide, it proved particularly successful in China and South Korea. There were a number of disasters—they couldn't get the online store running for a month, so there was no revenue at the outset—but they knew things looked bright. Today, *League of Legends* has more than a hundred million players playing month by month. And the store is indeed up and running. Because it is free to play, *LoL*, as it is known, makes money by in-game "microtransactions." In the past, the most common model was individual games sold for consoles: you bought your Xbox or PlayStation for a few hundred dollars, then paid $29.95 for *Grand Theft Auto* or *Call of Duty*. Then you paid the same amount, a few years later, for *Grand Theft Auto 2*. And a new console, after a while. And so on. (This is still a tremendously viable model, but it is no longer the only model.) A free-to-play game makes its money along the way, in smaller bites: in-game purchases. Players buy cosmetics and clothing for the characters, known as "skins." In 2017, *League of Legends'* revenue—bits of money collected just from making your video game character look cooler—was $2 billion.

What they also did by not releasing a *League of Legends 1, 2, 3*, and so on, was to keep designing and releasing what they had made new all along: the game changed slightly every few weeks. Minor tweaks, different abilities, entirely new champions: rather than just fix a few bugs and design an entirely new game for an eventual sequel to be sold separately, they transformed the living game as an evolving entity.

Today, with one-hundred-thousand users having become one-hundred-million users, Riot now has over two thousand employees in over twenty offices around the world. A great number of them are dedicated to continuing to develop that same entity—by now, most of the cells in the body have been shed and replaced and shed and replaced a thousand thousand times. All these years later, the company still tweaks the game every two weeks, called a "patch." Once a year they introduce more major changes—the map might change, or the terrain. Again and again, and again and again and again, over ten years of the game: What would make it more fun? This—or that? That—or this? In these constant updates, the *LoL* designers are paying close attention to what their players are telling them in real time. In fact, if you asked the entire design crew to make a list of the most important qualities for a good game designer, I think every single one of them would include some version of this concept: a good game designer has empathy.

A good game designer is always thinking some version of the following: What would someone who is not me enjoy in this situation? What would someone who is not me not enjoy in that situation?

With that in mind, one of the most important things to get right at the outset was matchmaking—when you started a game, what sort of teammates would you have? Could you bring your friends along? The design team wanted to make sure that they got it right, since they felt much of the toxicity in the personal online dynamics in gaming had to do with mismatched players, alone in a world of strangers. In *Warcraft III*, for instance, you went in alone or with a team of five. If you only had one friend, you were out of luck. In *League of Legends*, Cadwell wanted you to be able to play with your friends even without a full team.

There is an easy irony in that the value of empathy is considered so intrinsic to this process, that having an ability to anticipate other people's needs and feelings is such a fundamental building block for game design. This irony lies in the contrast between that care for others and the rest of the world's most negative perceptions of video game players. The notion that too much time spent on games leads to addiction and antisocial behavior is an entrenched complaint. About nine hundred years ago, for instance, the philosopher and theologian al-Ghazali, in *The Alchemy of Happiness*, wrote: "A person who has become habituated to gaming with pigeons, playing chess, or gambling, so that it becomes second-nature to him, will give all the comforts of the world and all that he has for those (pursuits) and cannot keep away from them." Politicians have gotten endless mileage out of suggesting video games are responsible for all manner of terrible acts, mostly to avoid talking about gun control or poverty or education. These perceptions, which you might boil down at its basest level to Stinky Antisocial Teenage Boy Bitterly Mauling and Trolling and Abusing Anything and Anyone in His Path from the Fetid Darkness of His Room, turn out to be a mostly inaccurate portrait of the gamer.

As it turns out, the average video game player is thirty-four years old. Seventy percent of gamers are eighteen or older; 45 percent of American gamers are women. And 60 percent of Americans play video games daily.

There is, as is often the case, a grain of truth to the stereotype. There are toxic players—trolls, dominators, and the like—and plenty of toxic culture, misogyny, casual cruelty, delight in sadism. Research has demonstrated that people do find it dramatically easier to treat each other evilly over the internet than they do in person. The most explosive episode in this sort of behavior gained a name in 2014—Gamergate. Gamergate began with a targeted campaign of online harassment of female game developers and game critics, and became more or less a digital culture war. To some, it represented the wider American argument about cultural standards and canons, diversification and privilege; to others, it was simply one side demanding an end to sexist, racist harassment in games, and greater inclusion in gaming, pitted against a mob of mostly misogynist trolls who felt threatened by the notion that games should be anything other than white men making games for white boys who liked to kill things on-screen.

The video game industry remains inordinately white, male, and straight. A survey conducted by the International Game Developers Association found that, of its respondents, 74 percent of game workers were cis males, 61 percent white/Caucasian/European, and 81 percent heterosexual. (Other studies have suggested that these numbers may be low, with as much as three out of four workers white and male.) Of the 963 respondents, only 1 percent of survey respondents identified as Black, African American, or African; 4 percent identified as Hispanic or Latinx; 23 percent identified as female; and 5 percent identified as transgender or "other." Without much design work coming out of non-white, non-male experience, you tend to get games that are born of white, male experience, obviously. These aren't numbers that differ vastly from the tech industry as a whole, but that doesn't make them any less dramatic.

Cadwell understands the numbers are dire, but he's also optimistic. For a young woman or a young person of color considering entering the field, the sea of white male faces might be daunting. But leaders in the industry want the way that sea looks to change, he said. "Within the field of design, I think the trend is positive and think there's been positive change since I've started," he told me, "even though there is a lot of work to do. I think we will see a lot of progress over the next few years, which is fueled both by companies seriously investing in diversity and inclusion, and players themselves being increasingly diverse as gaming is more broadly adopted as an activity. If you look at, like, the faces of active, serious players today, you'll see a group that's way, way, way, way more diverse than it was ten years ago, and certainly twenty years ago. Most game designers (and game developers as well) are serious players before they enter the industry, so a more diverse player community provides the talent that in turn can create a more diverse game industry and game design community. Those two factors together create the outcome."

In addition to it being the right thing to do, he said, there are also obvious benefits to increasing diversity. "I'd also say that knowing your audience is key to design, and teams that can be more diverse have advantages at understanding broader audiences more easily," he added. "I see this all of the time on my teams."

That said, the gaming industry does not have a sparkling track record on gender equity. And in 2018, two women, a Riot employee and a former employee, brought a class-action lawsuit against the company, asserting gender-based discrimination in pay and promotion, as well as a hostile work environment. In 2019, Riot agreed to a payment of $10 million to be distributed among one thousand employees, though only after two hundred current employees staged a walkout in Santa Monica. Then, in early 2020, the California Department of Fair Employment and Housing, which had launched its own investigation, released a statement saying that the women of Riot Games could be entitled to "over $400 million" in potential back pay, and the Department of Labor Standards Enforcement sued to intervene. The plaintiffs retained new counsel, who rejected the $10 million; as of this writing in March 2020, the case continues.

Naomi McArthur, a senior game designer at Riot, started work on *League of Legends* in the analytics department, doing business intelligence data modeling statistics for the player behavior team. Put as broadly as possible: What were the numbers saying about how the players conducted themselves in the game? The mandate of the team was to make the players nicer to each other, to create a safer in-game community. To that end, they built an array of machine-learning algorithms to build models to determine what experiences were leading to negative behavior. McArthur had studied computational neuroscience at Caltech (she described it as "bioscience and a little bit of psychology mixed with kind of a machine-learning statsy background, blended together in a weird weird combination"), and considered entering a PhD program to study neural systems, but she was also a gamer—she'd played *League of Legends* almost since its creation—and found herself attracted to making games.

She found entry initially through the *LoL* community boards. By then she also had some friends at Riot and sent in a résumé on a lark, and was thrilled to be hired as an analyst. After a few years on the analytics team, she moved into design, having been given the chance by a mentor to get a little practice at it. She worked originally on the champion design team—creating the new characters players got to choose—and was now working on a new game in development. One of the primary things she was thinking about was: In making a new game, what design choices will promote goodwill between players without removing the joy of competition and challenge? What engenders trust between strangers on the internet? How much should each player have to rely on another to succeed?

Trust is indeed a key factor. As Raph Koster, the game designer and creative director behind the MMORPGs *Ultima Online* and *Star Wars Galaxies*, has written, one example of a game design choice to engender trust is that a game should rely heavily on "blind moves." He says: "The design definition here is a move where one player executes a move or task that is a vitally required element to success," but that move only accomplishes half of what is required. Moreover, that player "*cannot see that the other player is there to 'catch it'* and execute the second half." Other strategies for creating a trusting game environment, he writes, include play where both players must do things in tandem; play where a player can only make moves for other players, and they can only make moves for him or her; games where there is restricted information flow between the players, each of whom must rely on their knowledge of the other player. You might design a game where you can't defend yourself, only others. One impediment to the success of this sort of game is that games that entirely rely on high-trust situations are almost impossible for novices, Koster points out, and are bound to be frustrating. In order to create something that new players can learn without tremendous effort, you need to allow them to switch from high-trust situations to low-trust— allow them to just rely on their own skills—at certain points within a game. Here is one of his solutions for that problem:

"Have classes and roles with unique abilities. Prevent a player from being good at the totality of the game with any given class. This is a tricky line to walk, since you want the game fully playable with any one class. But you also have to aim for a low *player efficiency*. This player shouldn't be able to crush the game, not by a long shot. If anything, as they hop around classes or roles, they should start to gain an appreciation for the varied roles other players would play in the ecosystem, and start to crave their presence. . . . Design your game with different roles, but don't make those roles overly hardcoded. Instead, design for strategic roles—dynamics, rather than mechanics."

This is something, it would seem, that *League of Legends* has done very well. Cadwell describes working for balance as a massive jigsaw puzzle—only the pieces haven't necessarily been cut exactly to the right shapes to fit in advance. The strengths and weaknesses of each character in each situation—and the number of situations becomes mind-boggling—have to arrive at a greater balance in toto, even if one situation might advantage one champion and another advantage an opponent. Otherwise, a small number of people will have fun and everyone else will mostly be miserable. The problems of evening things out gets even more complex when considering the vast differential in players' skill levels.

John Frank, a designer on the Summoner's Rift team ("the players know us as the 'balance team,'" he told me), came to Riot from a legal career—he practiced as a lawyer at a boutique firm, mostly doing contracts. In a way, he sees what he does as part of a much larger contract between Riot and the players: that the designers will always keep the universe of Runeterra in alignment. "There's hundreds of pros around the world and so we also need to balance for them," he said, "which throws a corkscrew in the mix, since the pro level is quite different from our normal game. So when we look at our buff and nerf list"—that is, the list of which champions to make stronger, and which to make weaker— "we see, oh, half of these nerfs we actually have to do because of the pro scene—if we were just looking at the data from the overall game, we wouldn't need to do this."

The professional e-sports scene, which has exploded over the last decade, is a vital component in the *LoL* world. The first *League* championships, in 2011, awarded $100,000 in prizes; now the prizes are in the millions, with millions of viewers. Players like Lee Sang-hyeok—"Faker"—are celebrities within the community. The e-sports industry, on its own, became a billion-dollar industry in 2019.

With this in mind, Riot designs what Frank called "very deep champions, which have many mechanics that are not immediately apparent," skills that take time and effort to master—many of which less-skilled players won't get to. But they also can't leave the less-skilled players with nothing. "If we were to balance entirely around the professional scene," he added, "the champions would feel so weak in the hands of the average player that they would feel punishing to play: they would feel totally underwhelming. So that's the tightrope."

Or rather, one of a hundred tightropes. Dan Emmons, who works as a designer on the champions team, described the process of creating a new character for me this way: "We release between eight and ten new champions a year. First we figure out: What is its place in the game going to be?" But to do that, they have to work on this from a number of angles: What's a cool way of playing that we're not currently supporting? But also: What is a group that isn't represented? What mechanics are being underused? What portion of the greater mythos of the game needs strengthening? "Once we get that hook, we put together what we call a core pod," Emmons said, "of a game designer, a narrative writer, and a concept artist, led by one of our production directors. And our job is to kind of take that core idea and spin it into what is the character going to be on a high level. So that's when I'm going to start working on individual abilities for the character, and how does it feel to play, what is the general role in the game going to be."

Emmons, like Frank, is one of many examples of designers who came from fields other than computer science or game design studies. Emmons studied electrical engineering in college, and playing games had just seemed like a fun hobby to him until he entered a design contest sponsored by Wizards of the Coast, a Seattle company that owns the rights to Dungeons & Dragons and makes the much-loved card game Magic: the Gathering. He didn't win the contest, but it sparked the idea that this could be a career, and after college he applied for a job in customer service at Wizards, and once with the company, looked for ways to move into helping to make the game. After a time in customer service, he was promoted to design; later, he'd go to Blizzard Games, and then to Riot. "The tools for making games are becoming way more widely accessible and generally more usable by people who don't have CS degrees," he told me.

Andrei van Roon, who is the *League of Legends* game director, said much the same. Van Roon grew up in New Zealand, where he studied geography in college and then did graduate work in transportation engineering and urban planning before working as a transportation engineer in Auckland for seven years. He was a *LoL* player, and in 2011 came across a notice Cadwell had posted on the boards that announced he was hiring for his design team. He applied. "I'd always been interested in game design, but given the lack of any meaningful industry in New Zealand at the time, and my lack of a coding background," he said—well, it was a nice dream. But Cadwell said in the post that he was looking for two types: recent CS graduates, and anyone with professional experience in another analytical field—meaning, more or less, the hard sciences, engineering, economics, and so on. *Well, that's me*, van Roon thought. During the interview process, Riot gave him about "a billion tests": What's wrong with this champion? Now can you design your own champion? How would you fix this problem with our new champion? How would you fix this problem with balance? And this? And that?

As it turned out, transportation engineering had prepared him to think in the way Cadwell was looking for. Or at least, what made him good at it also made him good at this. The idea is that the sharp systems thinking that people have been trained for in other disciplines is transferrable. About Cadwell, for instance, van Roon said, "I think Tom often thinks from an abstract perspective about game design, which is rare and valuable. What are the underlying principles that matter here that we should bear in mind always? That we should be building around? It makes him particularly strong at things like systemic design or building foundations. What are the principles by which content should be built? I think the systemic foundations side of things is the hardest skill set to find or to train."

With that in mind, Cadwell sought out not just designers from other companies or design schools, but a collection of tinkerers and searchers. When you are required to think about all the pieces of a puzzle and how shaping them will affect all the other pieces and form a whole, it makes sense that someone who's thought about these types of problems in other contexts might be good at design. "My work was on really long-term systems designed for Auckland, primarily," van Roon told me. "So for instance, I was looking at, if we put a freeway over here, well, twenty years from now, where do people end up living? How does that change traffic patterns? What effect do we expect that to have on the economy? What's the environmental impact?" How does one part of the system transform the whole?

That said, computer science itself attracts its share of people who like to investigate systems and think about patterns, of course. Christina Norman, who started as a lead designer at Riot in 2011, did her degree in mathematics and computer science. As a child, she taught herself to program, and made her first game at the age of eight. "The first game I made, you were in a maze and you wandered around and you'd encounter a dragon," she told me. "Then you'd have to answer a simple math problem. And if you answered it right, you killed the dragon. Otherwise the dragon killed you. It wasn't bad."

She came to Riot from the Canadian game developer Bioware, where she had been lead gameplay designer, after beginning her career working on software for startups. But she'd played *League of Legends* almost from the start—she holds the 301st assigned player ID—and her entry to the world of game design in part came though contacts she'd made as a player of games, the communities she'd found playing *Everquest* and *World of Warcraft*, as well as *LoL*. Since 2016, she had worked on new projects, in particular *League of Legends: Wild Rift*, redesigning the game for mobile and console versions. But her first job on League, she said, wasn't strictly game design. She was hired as creative director, in charge of creating a structure for the narrative world of Runeterra. "What I was really laying down was just the simple architecture of saying, 'What is the world of *League of Legends* like?' There was a series of stories and events, but there wasn't an underlying structure." The balancing trick was to create a structure to bind together a universe as a cohesive whole, a narrative that made sense and felt complete without creating constraints that would interfere with what the game could do. As it turns out, this sort of systems thinking has a wide applicability.

Buiko Ndefo-Dahl came to Riot straight out of Harvey Mudd College in 2015, armed with a CS degree and a lot of ideas. As a kid, playing *Pokémon* and *Super Mario 64* and others, he'd find himself coming to some understanding, he said, like, "Oh, here's a system; I've seen this system in other games—it could be an inventory system, for example, or a collectible system—I've seen it in four different games now. Surely they think there's something to this. But this one is so much better than the other ones. Why is it better? Why? This thinking soon became complaining about things, wishing things were better. All of my friends are surely exhausted by now of listening to me say, 'This game is good—but why did they do this? They could have just taken this system from over here, or they could have just simply changed this one facet of the design, and this would clearly be such a superior experience.'"

At twenty-seven, Ndefo-Dahl is one of the younger

designers—he works on the balance team—and grew up with video games, including the game he now works on. I asked him about the alchemy of fun—all these granules, these hundred million tiny parts fitting together to make one fun thing. "Ultimately, we craft experiences for people and we take nothing—that is, we take lines of code—and we turn them into concepts," he said, "and into a game world that players attach to and interact with, and experience. It's giving people an experience. Sometimes entertaining, sometimes meaningful, sometimes both, but either way, these individual parts have to coalesce into an experience. Not fun. It's not fun. Whenever anyone says games are about fun, they're wrong."

"Really?" I said.

"They *can* be fun," he said. "But fun is overrated. That would be a common sentiment around here. Because fun by definition is fleeting. If something's just fun, then you'll do it, and do it, until it's not fun anymore. Why do people play a sport? They play it for the feeling of mastery and improvement and teamwork. It actually rings alarm bells for me when I test something and people say: 'It was fun!' How was it fun? To me, if you don't understand where the fun is, there's a good chance where it's coming from is not something that's lasting and deep, but just novelty. Novelty doesn't last. Mastery, learning, meaning: they last. *League of Legends* is an infinite hill of mastery."

In fact, all the designers I met steered me away from stopping at fun. Van Roon said, "Most game design for me boils down to what are the actions and decisions you're offering the player, and what are the emotional opportunities you're giving them to engage with." And early on, Cadwell said, talking about his childhood and adolescence: "In retrospect, I did spend a lot of time on bad time-waster games."

"What's a time-waster? What makes a game that doesn't waste your time?" I asked.

"I guess it just depends on how new it is to you," he said. "Then, maybe those games were new to me—but now I see that this here is just a naked Skinner box that doesn't give me higher meaning; it just gives me a sense of progress, and maybe a little bit of exploration."

"Higher meaning?" I asked.

Cadwell gave me a subtle look.

Higher meaning! What does it mean for a game to have higher meaning? And once you know that, how do you design it?

5

HOW TO MAKE A MAGIC CIRCLE

How do you make a video game to begin with? Here is the standard path: A game starts with an idea, that idea is developed into a design, and that design gets implemented—with programming, with story, with art, with sound. Along the way that idea will change, develop, evolve. But that first idea might be a genre, a setting, a story, a set of rules someone wants to try. Above all, an idea eventually needs to include how the game works, what it will ask of the player, how it will allow the player to answer. That's the core design. One person may do it all, or there may be a team of one hundred. The design is, strictly speaking, separate from scripting, or programming, or the writing or the art or the sound, though of course each piece affects the others, and if one person is doing it all, well then, it's all of a piece. But first, once some of the idea has taken real shape, the next step is usually a prototype.

A game developer might use a preexisting tool, a game engine, which could be a proprietary program a big company has built for itself, or something premade that you can buy, software like Unity, Construct, or GameMaker Studio. That's scripting. It may be necessary to give it to an engineer next, if you're not doing it all yourself, who will take care of the more complex programming; there might be someone else in turn, if you're getting really fancy, in charge of thinking about how an AI component will work, making the physics of the world work, making the perspective work. An artist will be working on how the world looks. The designer—or, if it's a team, a team of designers he or she is overseeing—will imagine levels and more levels. Someone will write any text the game needs, any dialogue, any backstory; someone will do the sound; and so on. It will be tested and tested and tested, and changed and changed and changed. The game designer can be something like a film director, but also at times a screenwriter, cameraman, special effects studio, editor, key grip, producer, and so on, or like an architect, but also like a contractor, plumber, electrician, and so on and so on. That is to say, a programmer is not necessarily a designer, though a designer could be a programmer. An artist or a writer is not necessarily a designer, though a designer could be doing the art and writing. In some contexts, you could call these different parts system design and content design. Game designers, that is to say, do a wide variety of things, beyond making the rules of the game: they might be designing characters, or levels, or puzzles, or even be in charge of art and animation. They may also write code, or manage the project. It might include some of the worldbuilding, storytelling, art, sound; it might include level design, user interface design, user experience design. But what's happening is above all the defining of a universe and its rules.

How do you learn all this? How do you learn to make a video game? What you will most often hear from game designers, if you ask them, tends toward the abstract; which, if you were feeling uncharitable, you might call not abstract, but vague; which, if you were feeling annoyed, you might call not vague, but useless. What you will hear is: you learn to make a game by making a game. And then doing it again. And again, and again, and again. What they mean is, repeat that a few hundred or a few thousand times, and eventually you'll get there—the best way to learn is by doing.

What does that mean, just make one? How do you start? There are some 6.5 million answers on the internet for you, and about a third of those are videos, so no need to read anything if you don't want to. And what's more, once you have an idea, there are simpler tools you can use without any programming experience: you could try looking up simple game creation software with names like Twine, or GameMaker, or Stencyl. Even with many of the more complex tools, you can probably teach yourself, though advanced technical skills with a computer may eventually be important to getting as far along as you'd like. For many designers, entry comes from the modding community: that is, start not by making a new game but by experimenting with making modifications to an existing one. Learn how things work, and learn how to make a thing, by first adding to a thing, taking away from a thing, transforming a thing. That will start to teach you how to do it. Then, when you're ready, make your own. And finally, once you've made your game, there are a thousand new ways to sell it, or give it away, on platforms like Steam, or your own website, or pitching it to a big company, though that's not game design—that's business.

All this makes a certain amount of sense, in context: it is not uncommon for the people who make games to be autodidacts by nature, people who like to figure out engines and clocks and software programs by taking them apart and putting them back together, trial-and-error style. (The age of YouTube and Google is made-to-order for the figure-it-out heuristics of this strategy, since many of the fundamentals of what there is to solve have been figured out and posted.) What's more, this style has as an analog to that essential thing designers call "iteration," or "iterative design," which mostly means constant testing and changing as the game is built.

There are less lonely roads, both mimicking traditional career paths and deviating from them. But even with the former, it's not quite as simple as the old way. Did you want to be a doctor? Yes: so you went to college, took organic chemistry, applied to medical school, interned, resided, and so on. Did you want to be a lawyer? An accountant? You knew what to do. But game design? What is game school? What is the path?

The curriculum for aspiring game developers is a tricky proposition, since not everyone can even agree about what a game is, let alone come up with any consensus about game-design terminology or a canon of texts. Degree programs exist, if not yet the typical path. A number of programs have popped up across the country over the last decade or two, from USC to NYU, from the University of Utah to the University of Central Florida, offering BAs, BFAs, and MFAs in game design.

But what exactly is there to learn, other than programming, other than learning to use the game script tools? Listen: think up a premise, or even a whole story, or, even better, take someone else's (*Tinker Tailor Soldier Spy the Game*: you are George Smiley! Left-click to drink the claret, right-click to take a long trudge on a Cornish cliff) or something from history (*Significant Defenestrations*: journey back to Prague in 1618 and throw royals out the window! Do you want to write your apologia in Latin or German?). Or just pick a tried-and-true genre, throw in some robot-dragons or Romanian spies or space cowboys, then have them fight, or give them obstacles. Pay a programmer or learn to program, so you can give life to the heroes and the obstacles, to the army of sadomasochistic penguins you eventually decided would be your players' avatars, program them to shoot fire out of their butts at their enemies, an army of super-intelligent but depressed walruses, throw in some levels and landscapes and a few surprises (the walruses have a killer whale to deploy! And it can fly!), and make a few more small decisions (Is the butt-fire red? Green? Maybe it's blue! Blue fire from the penguin butts. Okay, shoot blue butt-fire. Die, walrus, die. Done!).

Eric Zimmerman teaches at NYU's Game Center, which offers both a Bachelor of Fine Arts and a Master of Fine Arts degrees in game design. "I teach the very first class students take," Zimmerman told me. "Game Design 1. Game design is like poetry, by which I mean, everyone thinks they can do it. Right? We all make up games, from childhood on. It should be easy. Especially if you take away the technical part. So the main thing is trying to get them to appreciate how hard it actually is."

A fork is a fork if it works: it's a fork if you can use it to put food in your mouth. A game is a game if it works—but what you use it for is less definable. "There's a whole host of cognitive skills necessary to make a game," Zimmerman said. That is, making a game also requires you to be a designer, yes, but also a mathematician, a logician, an artist, a storyteller, an anthropologist: what you're doing is not moving food from plate to person, but providing an experience. Frustration and relief, excitement and release. Something concrete and mechanical, something transcendent and ineffable.

Zimmerman, who is fifty-one years old, has been designing games for more than a quarter century. In 2000, he co-
founded Gamelab, a game development company in New
York City that hit success with a game called *Diner Dash* (you
run a diner, basically; it's one of the best-selling downloadable
games of all time) and Gamestar Mechanic, a site that lets
kids create games, which was funded by the first major game-
related grant from the MacArthur Foundation. He studied
art at the University of Pennsylvania—he was a painter—but
found the instruction stifling. (There is no meaning! There
is only color, line, and composition.) "In painting I felt I was
reshuffling a deck that had been handed to me by history," he
said. So he branched out into installations and performance
art, becoming interested in different kinds of interaction with
the viewer. And, eventually, interested in what the viewer
could do, him- or herself, with the art. This led him to games.

He had been a player of video games, as well as role-
playing games like Dungeons & Dragons, but hadn't considered the practice of making them as a career path. That
changed. "With games, suddenly I felt here's a cultural
form that's really reinventing its own possibilities: 2–D
games are becoming 3–D games, single-player video games
are becoming multiplayer video games. It just seemed like

a space that was full of a possibility." He went off to Ohio State to do an MFA in what was then called "Media Arts," and then on to New York to work at RGA Digital Studios, working on CD-Rom games. An avant-garde art piece turned out to be his way in: "They really hired me because I had done this project with a couple of colleagues in grad school which was called Arm the Homeless," he said. "It was a media hoax: a fake organization that claimed to give firearms and firearm safety training to homeless people. We had a Santa Claus collecting money. They loved it."

He also began teaching, with fellow game designer Frank Lantz, at NYU's Interactive Telecommunications Program (ITP), which was generally described as "art school for engineers." It was a pretty wide-open field. "We were not the first people to ever try to teach people game design, but it was very rare," Zimmerman said. "And so there weren't a lot of models. We really had to invent what does it mean to teach a class in this."

Part of what it meant to teach a class in game design had to do with the necessity of creating and identifying philosophies, concepts, and canon, since nobody had really defined any of the terms. In many ways, that's only beginning to change now. There is still no universal grammar of game design: different developers use different vocabularies and structures. The concepts and principles of game design remain vague and contradictory and without consensus, and only a first generation of any critical theory or language about gaming exists. The difficulty of teaching a class in game design also had to do with how variable games are, and the variable notions of what a game is supposed to do. What a game is supposed to be. In his foundational book *Rules of Play*, which Zimmerman wrote with a colleague, Katie Salen, they begin this process by saying that a game is a system in which players engage in an artificial conflict, defined by rules, in which there is a quantifiable outcome. But this is a definition that leaves a lot of room for stretching the boundaries.

Today, the Games 101 class at NYU covers "advanced game literacy," which is to say "the development of a shared understanding of the history of games, culturally and aesthetically." It's an intro survey: building a critical vocabulary, understanding the history, analyzing games' formal and structural properties. It begins with chess and Go and soccer and stretches on to *Super Mario Bros.* and *Half-Life*. Zimmerman teaches a class called "Survival Skills" as well, an overview of the professional possibilities in game design, starting with a different tranche each week of the industry: the Indie Path (working alone or in small teams on independent projects); the Media Company Path (career paths in non–game media companies); the Studio Path (finding and landing a job at a game development company). The course also addresses getting a job or starting a company—résumés and cover letters, portfolios and internships, entrepreneurship and fund-raising—and alternatives to commercial game-making, which is to say, largely, academia and the art world.

Game design is a growth industry. That's not to say the starting salaries will make anyone rich. The pay for entry-level jobs varies by region and type of company, but ranges from around $45,000 up to $85,000 at the larger companies (in part because there are so many more candidates for these jobs than there are positions). Mid-level designers, a few years in, might make in the low six figures, and six or seven years in perhaps around $150,000. (Again, the industry varies so widely that these numbers are hardly cast in stone.) Leadership positions start to move the needle upward. At the large companies—say, Epic, which makes *Fortnite*, or Rockstar, which makes *Grand Theft Auto*, or Activision Blizzard (*World of Warcraft*), or King (*Candy Crush*)—just getting through the door can be an incredibly competitive atmosphere. That said, the industry is growing at a terrific rate, and the number of jobs will only increase.

Riot Games also offers a course in the basics, through its URF Academy, which is aimed at high school and middle school students, and offers its curriculum free of charge as a teaching tool. (It was created, in part, as an aid to diversify the talent pipeline: to reach students early on who might not have had the same opportunities for exposure to gaming and design.) The curriculum lays out of a set of fundamental elements of game design, in six modules, based on the notion that games typically have these following core features: a player; a goal; meaningful decisions and opposition; rules and thematics; and interaction. Over the six modules, the curriculum goes over things from mechanics ("Mechanics are essentially the rules that allow players to take, or not take, actions and make decisions in a game") to a model for eight kinds of fun (sensation, fellowship, challenge, fantasy, narrative, discovery, expression, and submission, all of which are fairly self-explanatory, though for the last one—submission—someone will have to explain slot machines).

So baseline ideas of how to teach design have begun to form, if in a somewhat decentralized way. One thing most people in the field do agree on is that modern study of play, for the world of games anyway, usually must begin with *Homo Ludens* (1938), the Dutch historian Johan Huizinga's treatment of the role of play alongside the formation of culture and society. The title, more or less, means "Man the Player": a kind of updating to the eighteenth-century coinage of *homo sapiens* (man the knower) and argument to *homo faber* (man the maker). (In the more academic reaches of the game world, you'll hear a lot of references to "ludology," the study of play.) "Play is freedom," Huizinga wrote, most famously, but perhaps just as foundationally, "The view we take in the following pages is that culture arises in the form of play, that it is played from the very beginning." Huizinga set out some of the fundamental characteristics of play, some of which have held up better than others, but have served for a century as a foundation for building and argument. Play, he said, is free; play is not ordinary life, but instead something unreal; play creates order, has rules; play has no profit or gain.

Modern games have complicated his definitions. Professional sports, for example, are in fact not without profit or gain, but surely remain games. Putting aside for the moment the very large idea that "games are free" or "games are freedom," it seems certainly true that a game needs rules to be a game. The point of football is to score more points than your opponent, for instance. If that was the end of it, you could just give your quarterback a flamethrower, send him out with it and the ball: he'd get you points that way. Hence: NFL rulebook rule 2346 b, no flamethrowers in the backfield. Or, if there is no such rule, there is certainly some language that is interpretable as including a no-flamethrower clause. A game requires these sorts of constraints. Bazookas for the tight ends, drone strikes in the secondary; this would make whatever was going on not football anymore.

So: "a game has rules" is pretty simple. But how about Huizinga's third rule, that play is not ordinary life, but an unreal space? Here is Huizinga's description: "The arena, the card-table, the magic circle, the temple, the stage, the screen, the tennis court, the court of justice, etc., are all in form and function play-grounds, i.e., forbidden spots, isolated, hedged round, hallowed, within which special rules obtain. All are temporary worlds within the ordinary world, dedicated to the performance of an act apart." Zimmerman has written extensively about this space, this temporary, special space that exists apart from our normal reality; he named it, using it as a general principle, "the magic circle." The magic circle, he told me, "is a finite space with infinite possibility." But what does that mean, infinite possibility? What, exactly, is an unreal space? And how do you make one?

Stone Librande, who is a lead designer at Riot, boiled down the problem for me. Librande lives in the Bay Area ("Riot North"), and also teaches a game design workshop for students in Carnegie Mellon University's Entertainment Technology Center. Riot's URF Academy curriculum is based on his college course. Students start with pen and paper, no other technology. This is in part because Librande believes the game mechanics are the core of the creation— he sees the overlay of technology as floors built over the foundation. Among the basic concepts in his course, he said, is the idea that "If you really think about playing a video game, brutally honestly, you're saying, 'I'm going to go home and I'm going to hold on to a piece of plastic and tap my thumb against the plastic while I look at colored lights change on a piece of glass.'" So the trick of the game is to convince you you're not just tapping plastic buttons on your couch: you're fighting aliens, you're shooting Nazis, you're building a farm, you're throwing a pass, you're shooting blue fire out of your butt. "That's the main video game design trick," Librande said. "How do you map aesthetics and feelings and emotions onto mechanical risk-reward, Pavlovian behavioral systems?"

That's part of the magic circle: you're a cowboy on a horse. For a time. For those moments, those hours, you're there: you're not sitting on a couch. You're in a saddle, in a magic space. The normal rules of life—the normal chaos of life—do not apply. Surely some of this is achieved with art and technology: extraordinary vistas, evocative music, angles of perspective, photo-realism, even virtual realities. But its foundation is in the mechanics of the game. Almost all the designers I met agreed that for all the story and art and technology, the simple core of what makes games games was providing the player with the act of making choices. Without that act, without the chance to make engaged decisions that affect how the experience proceeds, you have a movie or a book or a painting that you are external to. You are not making decisions about where the book or movie will go. You may create, with the author, a virtual text in your head, based on your imagination and the author's words, but you cannot choose whether or not Anna Karenina is going under that train.

I'd mentioned earlier to Librande that it had taken me until the age of twenty-eight to, at long last, beat my father at chess. "If you think of that game of chess, when you finally beat him," Librande said, "it's very possible you weren't thinking about anything else. Your whole brain was in that game: you weren't thinking about what you were going to eat later or watch on TV, you were thinking about what move did he just make and what move will I be making, you had no room in your brain to think about anything else except the pattern and sequence of moves. You were completely immersed in chess to a degree that you weren't thinking that you were sitting in a chair at a table pushing wooden pieces around a black-and-white grid. And this is not a real-world analog: it's a chess world, just moves and shapes and patterns."

So, again: what the game designer is doing is providing some tangible thing, whether it be physical or digital—a grid, eight-by-eight squares, or a hundred yards of turf or four bases on a diamond of dirt or an underground lair of zombies—and within the frame of that thing, providing rules and populating it with choices that will draw a person into that thing, to live in that thing for a while, to have a real experience within the constructed circle that is defined by its rules as different from the outside world. So this circle is created by its rules: by the mechanics of the game, as well as the aesthetics of the game, the story of the game, and the technology of the game.

But what exactly is happening in that circle? What immerses us? A good story draws you in, fires up your imagination. Beautiful art can do the same. Sound charges an emotional response, fills out a consuming space. But what about the mechanics of the game? Obviously it's important for games that we are physically implicated in some way—you need to move the joystick or press the button. All you need to do is watch kids playing arcade games, ducking and twisting as if they were inside the machines, to see how much that matters. The psychologist Mihaly Csikszentmihalyi, who coined the term "flow," or "flow state," to describe that state of complete concentration and absorption, describes this experience as "being completely involved in an activity for its own sake. The ego falls away. Time flies. Every action, movement, and thought follows inevitably from the previous one, like playing jazz. Your whole being is involved, and you're using your skills to the utmost."

Raph Koster, in his book *A Theory of Fun for Game Design*, argues that fun in games essentially consists of the feedback the brain gives us when we are learning something. The brain is identifying patterns, and then having learned how the patterns work, following them and anticipating them with increasing mastery. Absorbing those patterns is what draws us in. The next step might be recognizing an unexpected pattern, or a change to the pattern—designers will have to figure out how much changing the pattern will draw us further in, and how much will toss us out. Either way, we are absorbing patterns and learning about them—but within the magic circle, and without obvious purpose other than entertainment.

And so what would make those patterns, that grid, that flick of the joystick, that choice to kill all the Nazis you see with a flamethrower and not a howitzer, meaningful? And what would it mean?

Zimmerman starts with the idea that all successful game design results in meaningful play. He says that meaningful play begins when the action of the player and that action's outcome have a relationship. Because this is a starting point for him that you can almost say about all games—you turn left, you get to eat the dots and get a cherry; you turn right, Blinky gets you, Ms. Pac-Man dies. The meaning of your decisions is pretty simple, but consequential all the same.

You eat enough to complete the challenge, level up, the ghosts get faster, and there are different rewards, and so on. But the chain of consequence your decisions as a player creates can be more complex and complete, or less.

So that's the simplest version of meaningful play: Is there a growing tree of consequence from your choices? As the tree grows, though, the range and scope of meaningful choices expands. And of course, those decisions don't take place in a vacuum, and meaning can't be restricted to a question of whether when you do something, something else happens that makes sense in the context of what you did. The choices you're making may be based in pattern-recognition pathways, there may be an unconscious higher mathematics taking place in your brain, but there is also a setting for those decisions: a story, a sound, a view. Koster points out that it would be a very specific experience to play a game that required you to fit the greatest number of murdered prisoners in a pit—you shoot them and toss them in, and whoever uses the geometry of the shapes and space best, and so tosses the most corpses in, wins—but if you consider this horrific hypothetical game just based on the meaning of its gameplay, it is in fact *Tetris*.

Consequence of mechanics, and cultural context, then,

to begin. But of course it's not quite that easy. "You know, what you find meaningful may not be what I find meaningful," Tom Cadwell told me. "Maslow's hierarchy is a very good description of a hierarchy that Maslow personally felt." (Abraham Maslow's famous pyramid is a five-tier model of human needs: health and food and sleep; safety; love and belonging; self-esteem; and self-actualization.) In general, though, Cadwell said, he's not averse to the idea that establishes three large categories for meaningful games—though he cautioned this was a simplification, and not including some of the latest thinking—which are first, mastery; second, community; and third, autonomy. How much can I improve my skills, learn to master these patterns? How can I find a group of people to do it with me, a group that will give me a feeling of belonging? Who am I? What can I do? What choices can I make?

Huizinga says all play means something: all play transcends itself. If this is true, that meaningful play is by nature transcendent, in some sense, then, this is a paradox. The game must first draw you into a magic circle, give you the sense that you are within this unreal world, that for the moment it is all there is; but for there to be meaning in play, if it must transcend itself, then that meaning in games has to do with what escapes the magic circle, goes beyond it. Mastery, community, autonomy must extend past the borders of this universe. Meaning is something more than the thing itself, the thing that means.

It might be learning that you take with you outside the circle, it might be mastering a skill, which you can apply in real life—throwing the rock at the tree was fun, but later it turns out you got good at throwing and hit more saber-tooth tigers with the rock and survived slightly longer than you would have otherwise. It might be the feeling of triumph or the experience of loss. It might be working with a group, or finding a community. It might be the experience of empathy for others; it might be the experience of losing your identity and trying on another, existing as something or someone else, or exerting power or falling victim to power; it might be catharsis, or an idealization of an imperfect world, or an experience of a distorted, demented one. You are drawn into a new universe, some kind of simulated Eden populated not with serpents and apples, but dragons and spaceships and soldiers and plumbers, only again to be cast out once you've learned something.

6

THE GARDEN OF FORKING PATHS

Riot Games employs an army to shape and reshape its juggernaut of a game, thousands of designers and engineers and executives hunkered down in Santa Monica and out across the world, a massive, interconnected hive of extremely complex and efficient labor bound together as a whole. Blendo Games, a few miles down the road from Riot HQ, in central Los Angeles, employs only one. Blendo is Brendon Chung; Brendon Chung is Blendo. (He has, for some games, contracted out some parts—the music on one game, some level design on others.) Chung's games comprise a mix of genres, but he is probably best-known for first-person puzzle-adventure games, made up of equal parts dry wit and strange dreams. Everybody who plays video games finds the genres that make them happiest, and for me—squarely in Generation X middle age, slowed in the reflexes and mostly disarmed of whatever youthful bloodlust I ever had in me, washed away by time—the puzzle-adventure game is it.

Chung himself is thirty-nine, an LA native—he grew up in San Gabriel, a small suburb—and he makes games that each mostly take place in a single specific, expanding universe of his own creation, giving the impression that with each game you are seeing a little more and more of a reality that exists beyond what your window into it has thus far allowed. He works out of a studio with a collective of other independent game designers and artists called Glitch City. Chung, though, is not entirely a fan of the label "indie games," because all the term means to him really is just video games made without the financing of a company or corporate publisher, so when someone says, "I like indie games!" it doesn't explain much about what it is they like.

As with so many game designers, what Chung liked, from childhood on, was making things—an early fascination with understanding systems, and transforming them, and eventually creating his own systems, and giving them life. "I really did like building things, I'd build things out of basically anything, I'd build things out of garbage," he told me. "We had these kabob sticks, skewer sticks, and I'd just take a bunch with a tube of glue—you can do a lot with that.

I was usually making little scale models. My pride and joy was a roller coaster. I built it and put a small steel marble on it, and then I'd experiment with it, rolling the marble down the skewers and taking little turns. Just a little wooden roller coaster. I was obsessed with theme parks; I was obsessed with Disneyland. This is pre-internet, so I would write a letter to every park that I could find in the world, across America, and ask them to send me a brochure with a map on it. I was obsessed with maps also. The combination of maps and parks drove me crazy."

Chung's uncle worked in computers, a network engineer, and in the late '80s he brought the family their first computer, an IBM XT, a ponderous, giant machine they set up in the living room. Chung and his brother and sister began fooling around with it, working out how to use DOS, until after a few weeks of that they figured out how to use the command C D, to enter directories, and found a directory their uncle had preinstalled: "GAMES." They found a hundred or so executable files, one new game after another.

"These games, I guess you could say they were pirated," Chung told me, "and this was back in the day when games did not have tutorials. And they didn't really teach you how to play them. I think sometimes they had manuals that came with the game, but we didn't have the boxes. So most of our time was spent just trying to figure out how the hell to play the game, what the rules were. Games back then were a lot more abstract and your avatar would just be a diamond or something like that, and we couldn't even tell what certain things were meant to be. So a lot of it was just spent trying to decipher what was happening. Who am I supposed to be? What is the goal of this? Why did I just die?"

Chung's sixth-grade yearbook had a section asking all the students what they wanted to be in the future; he put down video game designer. By that time, he was already trying to build his own things, as well as trying to tweak existing games, create mods. His video game programs first took shape in QBasic, which stands for Quick Beginners All Purpose Symbolic Instruction Code: a programming language software that came with example programs to teach you how to use it, including *Nibbles*, a navigation game involving a snake, and *Gorillas*, which pits gorilla against gorilla hurling bananas at each other. "The only thing I was able to make," Chung said, "were incredibly awful text adventure games where everything you do, you die, basically."

In high school, he made a mod for the game *Quake 2* (a first-person shooter game) called *Citizen Abel* using a free download of the official software editor for the game, which, in a pre-YouTube era, he taught himself to use reading tutorials and community boards online. It attracted notice from *Quake 2* players, and for the first time he experienced what it was like for strangers to find a thing you made, and to use it and discuss it and enjoy it.

In *Citizen Abel* you ran around at the behest of nefarious employers with a shotgun, depositing chunks of people around the screen. Chung liked the first-person games—he also played lots of *Doom*, another shooter—but he was also attracted to building types of games, like *Sim City*, and point-and-click adventure games. Around that time, the filmmaker George Lucas had founded a small game studio, and their new adventure games appealed to him. Old-school design, according to Chung, was often just mean: you killed things, or you died, and if you died, you lost your progress. Or you made a mistake early on and three hours later discovered that that mistake you couldn't have known you were making now prevented you from moving forward, and you were just stuck.

"LucasArts did away with all of that stuff," he told me. "You can never die. You can't screw yourself over. And they were really funny, and really charming, and had lots of per-

sonality. It was a very new fresh thing in adventure games."
As someone who played a lot of games, it wasn't that Chung
wanted games to be easy, but he did like the more forgiving
philosophy of this new wave. A game design didn't need to
be unkind, he felt, to be challenging and interesting.

He went to college at UC San Diego, hoping to make
video games for a living, but didn't find a clear academic
path in game design. A computer science major seemed too
academic and theoretical for his purposes. He ended up with
a major in visual arts, concentrating on film, where he was
struck by a new wave of independent movies, like Robert
Rodriguez's *El Mariachi*, which Rodriguez made for seven
thousand dollars, and Wong Kar-Wai's *Chungking Express*.
"A person made this," Chung said. "I felt, this is so beautiful, but it also felt like a person could get a camera and make
something happen." Without a corporate machine behind it.

He wrote screenplays and plays and stories and made
"weird little things with my friends," short films, experiments. All along, he was still experimenting with his own
mods and games, extending *Citizen Abel*'s adventures, which
introduced the world to the universe of Nuevos Aires. (In
one, Abel becomes a genetically designed super-assassin
in infancy: you play a machine-gun-toting baby, rewarded

for kills with cookies and milk.) Upon graduation in 2004, he put his game design work on a CD-Rom and shipped it to every game company he could find on the internet. At first, nobody wanted to hire him without professional experience. It took him a year to find work, when Pandemic Studios (where Tom Cadwell had interned while at MIT) offered him a job as a level designer. "It was a lot of luck," he said. Pandemic did mostly console games; Chung had played and worked on PCs, and it was a new set of skills to learn. But they liked a mod he had made for *Half-Life* that showed his skill at creating coordinated squad maneuvers, which, as it happens, was the kind of action that took place in their biggest games. He had no professional experience, but by then Pandemic had begun hiring people from different fields, looking for talent as much as skill: Chung's colleagues included a former TV cameraman, a former bartender, a former music promoter.

The big change for Chung was going from doing everything himself—the vision and the design, the story and the landscape, not to mention coding, scripting, sound, and art—to working on a team. He enjoyed it. "The things that a team can do are just so much exponentially more than what any one individual person could do," he said. "It's not that two people can do twice as much work, it's that two people can do four times as much. And there's a great feeling about being a part of a team and making work together. Like seeing a giant machine where all the pieces work together. It's pretty satisfying."

The first game he worked on was called *Full Spectrum Warrior* 2, which he describes as "military people doing military things." Pandemic put him in charge of the tutorial level, the first level the player plays, which essentially teaches him or her how to play the game. This suited him well. Because the tutorial level has a lot of intricate detail work—it has to set up the whole game, teach the player the general outline of how to handle any upcoming situation—he got a wider experience in the aspects of design and game development than he might have otherwise, working closely with different departments, programmers, artists, and writers, and began to understand the jigsaw puzzle from a wider view. "Whatever you touch on your end will be touching a bunch of other people's work," he said.

Chung worked at Pandemic for five years, working on such games as *The Lord of the Rings: Conquest*. While at Pandemic, he began creating his own game on his own time. As much as he liked working with a team, he also missed working on games that came entirely out of his own head. That project, Chung said, was an experiment: a first-person shooter without shooting. "When I start a project, I like to give myself limitations," Chung said. "I think it helps focus a project and steers it in a very clear direction." In this case, he didn't allow himself any shooting and didn't allow any dialogue. How could you make a first-person shooting game without any shooting? How could you tell a story without any dialogue?

"When you're first just learning how to make anything, just making the pieces that make the thing come together is hard to do," he said. "And really it continues to be hard. And why not just copy *Space Invaders* or *Asteroids* or *Pong*? Even making *Pong* is incredibly challenging when you're starting from scratch. But eventually you want to make something that hasn't existed before. And I had finally gained the tools in the toolbox to make the things I wanted to do. Make things that didn't already exist."

He was doing it on his own time, so in a sense the stakes were low, since nobody was throwing out money and expecting a return from his eventual product, and he wasn't relying on the game for a paycheck. He finished it in 2008, using the open-source game engine for *Quake 2*, and called it *Gravity Bone*. *Gravity Bone* extended the world of Nuevos Aires, a fantastic city-state sometimes reminiscent of an imaginary South American capital, a sleepy Caribbean metropolis, some hidden urban sprawl of a fabulous past banana republic that never existed, and then sometimes something of an entirely different order, a glimpse of a future world or alternate past. The opening begins with a bit of text—the beginning of his project of tying one glimpse of a big universe in one game to another glimpse in another game—that gives you a sense of what kind of place you've come to. It's titled "Citizen Abel":

There is a bullet hole in the Marca Registrada Club in Nuevos Aires. Of the hundreds of patrons who filter through the club every night, there are always several In The Know. In their minds, they relive the moment Citizen Abel stepped foot into the Marca Registrada and unleashed forty-five caliber improvisation upon the Digsy-era New Musical Dinette Gang.

As far as I can tell, you will never be entirely In The Know, no matter how many times Chung allows you into Nuevos Aires. You didn't see Citizen Abel shooting up any Dinette Gang, whoever they are. You don't know quite where you are, exactly, and once you do, to some extent, you start to have a sense that there is a lot of life going on and a lot of history that has gone on that exists beyond your vision. You don't know quite who you are, either—not completely, anyway. But as the narrative through-line of the games continues, a gathering cloud of hints and clues and fragments and vignettes starts to take form. Feeling precedes knowledge; you start to put together a picture of this universe yourself, as if you arrived here as a stranger and gradually came to know some portion of the history and culture and customs through overheard pieces and stolen witness. It's an evocative world—it feels not like an incomplete one pretending to be complete, but rather like a complete one that has only offered you an incomplete view thus far.

Gravity Bone starts as you arrive at the Saturday Club, a set of vertiginous chalet terraces overlooking snowcapped mountains. It's a bright day, with bright colors—yellows and blues—the kind of light you might imagine to be able to see in the Andes. Waiters serve drinks. The guests ignore you; the men wear tuxedos; the women are all in black dresses. Everyone is wearing a black mask and has a rectangular body and a disproportionately large square head. Your first job is to get your assignment from the furnace room, which requires sneaking through the kitchen and collecting a drink and a waiter's uniform. The level could be considered a tutorial, teaching you how to navigate—how to open doors, how to jump and duck at the right times. When you complete your assignment, delivering a doped drink to the man with red hair, your contract is fulfilled, and you'll get $1,000 base payment, plus various bonuses, including $300 Phantom Pants Bonus, $100 Zero Emissions Bonus, and $100 All Teeth Intact Bonus. The music is rumba; the mood is insouciant; the payment means nothing. There is no shooting, and nobody talks to you.

It's on the second level (there are only two—it's a short game) that Chung subverts the expectations of the player that he's set up. Mostly what you have to do there is break locks and take photographs of birds. "I think at that time first-person games were mostly about having M-16 rifles and space aliens and stuff like that," he said. "So I was mostly just having fun playing with those tropes and genres." The game dissolves, transforms itself, and takes the control you thought you had achieved away from you, and in so doing gently points out the conventions of games, the things gamers take for granted, by frustrating them. It has proposed a rhythm and a progression that people who play video games are used to, and then denied that expectation. A lady you had assumed was just another bot, useless to you for good or ill, suddenly shoots you, takes your camera, and escapes. You follow her, but without much recourse. You thought you had learned a rule and could forget about it, follow it without thinking each time, but the rule suddenly changes. The fee you collected offers you no help: you can't buy more lives, or strength, or health. You cannot escape your fate. How to level up, how to win, how to master the game: these are beside the point. So what is the point, if not winning? Is it still a game if there is no winning or losing?

Meanwhile, in 2009, not too long after he shipped *Gravity Bone*, Chung lost his job. Pandemic Studios went under. He'd been working on a new game in the same Nuevos Aires universe, *Atom Zombie Smasher*, but he realized that it wasn't ready, and that he had no way to fix it: the code was a jumble, and he didn't know how to unjumble it. "This was when I learned the term 'technical debt,'" he'd write later, in the notes at the end of the game when it finally did ship. "It's what happens when you choose to take quick-n-dirty shortcuts. Makeshift hacks are certainly alluring—they get you short-term results incredibly quickly and you feel like the most productive person on the planet. But these quick hacks add up and you end up paying for it." He'd learned to code by looking at code, combing through the lines that make up *Quake*, that make up the game *Half-Life*, "poring over it, kind of changing numbers and seeing what happens and ripping my hair out because I had no idea what I was doing." Then he had used tutorials to teach himself the language C#. Now he was in technical debt. The game wasn't going to work, and he was unemployed.

Not sure that he could support himself by opening his own shop, he began looking for a new job. But he also started making *Flotilla*, a space-combat strategy game that pits your fleet of massive battleships in space against enemies. Instead of the more typical, nimble rocket fighters in other games, you have to plan for these massive spaceboats' lumbering movements. The music is Chopin; the strange dreams are intact (you can pick up a space panda named Shaba, not that it changes much). *Flotilla* was released in 2010 and gave him just enough money and space to keep working. He decided to start his own company: Blendo Games.

He returned to *Atom Zombie Smasher* the following year, which in turn returned us to Nuevos Aires. It has, since our last visit, been overrun by zombies. It is January 1961; the music is surf rock; the view is from top-down, ten thousand feet above. The mood is a mix of comic-book guilelessness and semi-ironic commentary: "Look, Gubo! Behind those trees . . . zombies!" As a member of the Nuevos Aires Orbital Command, you are tasked with evacuating the city. Chung put the player in the role of a hero who has to do awful things for the greater good. To save humanity, you had to come to realize that you had to sacrifice a few civilians—or more than a few. You start off burning zombies, but at some point you have to face the fact that you are going to have to burn some humans, too. Meanwhile, to encourage players to mess with what he'd made, Chung allowed for the game rules to be changed however you liked, and encouraged players to share their mods through the Online File Share.

"That's kind of a unique thing with games, that you share some authorship of a thing with the player," he told me. "First, a player has such a big influence on what actually happens, obviously, and so because of that, as a developer you either have to just double down and try to control it harder, or let it go and open yourself up to just letting the player be part of it. I think something really, really magical happens when you do just let the player make connections on their own. And then the game gives them the breathing room to play around and discover new things on their own."

Next up was *Thirty Flights of Loving*, a kind of sequel to *Gravity Bone*. Another first-person shooter without guns (or at least, without guns for you), and also relatively short, it stars the player as a spy again, though this time you have two confederates: Anita and Borges. Anita (Demolitions; Mechanic; Sharpshooter; Confectioner) has a robot arm and a square head, and maybe loves you; Borges (Forger; Safecracker; Pilot; Best Man) has squinty eyes and a black beard, and a first name (Winston). There are cases of Midnight Hobo Vodkahol to drink, an array of unbothered ducks and cats, a wedding party, a shootout you somehow arrive at after it's over, an airport, and plenty of inside jokes and authorial mythologies. As in *Gravity Bone*, players are thrown into a context their avatar knows much more about than the players do—that is, you've been dropped into a narrative that began before you arrived and is moving ahead at great pace and what you see now only evokes a whole life that's gone on before as you hurtle into the future. There's love, and betrayal, there's the scope of a whole life glimpsed through fragments and images, a fractured collage of an existence. The game makes you do some of the imaginative labor to construct a narrative, but it's there for you to come to as you will.

Chung was thinking a lot about what sort of control a player can have over a game. To what extent could you say, here are some rules, and then, within those rules, you're entirely free? Was that freedom fictional? Do the constraints of the game control you more than you think? How can a player be freer, short of the impossible feat of programming an infinite universe? For his next game, Chung created a Nuevos Aires world where you write the code yourself.

"Growing up, my dad worked on cars, and did carpentry and plumbing and electric work," Chung said. "He was one of those guys who just kind of did everything. And it's really very memorable for me, helping him do all these things, and I wanted to make a game to play with those things, those physical things that you can use to affect the world. And I tried to marry that with the other big thing in my life, which was computers—not contemporary computers, but the computers I grew up with, DOS and command prompts."

Out of this came *Quadrilateral Cowboy*. It's a heist adventure puzzle game: you, as Poncho, must penetrate security systems with the gray-market tools of the trade. "When you have a top-of-the-line hacking deck," he writes in the game's tag line, "armed with a 56.6k modem and a staggering 256k RAM, it means one thing: you answer only to the highest bidder." The game, significantly longer and deeper than Chung's previous games, took four years to build.

Most video games direct you pretty clearly toward their source material. J. R. R. Tolkien's long shadow is overrepresented, it's fair to say. The influence of Buck Rogers and Star Trek and Star Wars is both wide and deep. Modern and historical warfare; horror movies; cartoons. With most of it, you can point to a few things as foundational, or sometimes a single source as fully responsible for the "intellectual property." With Chung, though, a backlit world of influences and echoes seems more like a web of kinship; his finished games often send you thinking of comparisons but arrive at something entirely original. He told me that the universe of Nuevos Aires owed something to a large array of things he liked, including Terry Gilliam's movie *Brazil*, a few different Wong Kar-Wai films, a 1990s Disney cartoon called *TaleSpin* that takes place in a sort of '30s art deco atmosphere. Often, his games made me think of writers: Julio Cortázar hopscotching; Georges Perec limiting himself to four vowels; Donald Barthelme's heartbreaking experiments; Philip K. Dick; Jules Verne; H. G. Wells; Jorge Luis Borges, everywhere and nowhere.

Quadrilateral Cowboy points a little more in one particular direction than the others, starting off back in a groove in the culture that William Gibson started cutting forty years ago or so. It might also remind you of later stuff—*Ghost in the Shell*, or *Snow Crash*—but in *Quadrilateral Cowboy*, as in *Neuromancer* (1984), Gibson's first novel, the plot follows a heist that takes place partly in physical space and partly in the matrix. (The coining of the term "the matrix" in this sense was Gibson's invention, as far as I can tell.) *Quadrilateral Cowboy* reaches back for some of the clunky newness of this '80s vision, that alternate technofuture that mostly happened but sometimes didn't. "The matrix has its roots in primitive arcade games," Gibson wrote, "in early graphics programs and military experimentation with cranial jacks."

But this is not a primitive arcade game. It's also not Gibson, but Chung. You're back in Nuevos Aires; the square heads, the wit, the feel; it's all personal and specific and recognizable. You enter *Quadrilateral Cowboy* on a hoverbike; on your portable Vinylman, the sound of "Clair de Lune." It's New Year's Eve 1979. The night sky is blue-black. You jump from your bike to a moving train for your first heist. Over the next few hours, you jump, crouch, shimmy, and cut your way into buildings and basements and towers, in the city and eventually in outer space, to steal what you've been contracted to steal. Once you're in cyberspace, you can launch yourself, saw through grates, and above all, hack your way past cameras and lasers—that is, by typing in code on the keyboards of your deck—manipulating the security features without setting off the alarm. (You begin by logging on to telnet and follow prompts before trying to get inventive. Laser1.off(3), for instance, will disable laser 1 for three seconds; the game more or less teaches you how to use the commands as you go.)

Figuring it out is sometimes easy, sometimes extremely difficult—I got stuck fairly often. It's a problem-solving series, and while being foxed by a puzzle can be frustrating, it requires you to become inventive, to think beyond the patterns that you've already seen. Meanwhile, you get to exist and examine the new reaches of this universe. As you progress, you can gather more useful tools—a rover for getting past unpassable obstacles, a CCTV kit for surveillance—and the jobs get more complex. There are eighteen levels, mostly assignments: for the Satsuma Job you must acquire a safe locked in a building; for the Abby Yoyo Space Elevator gig you must acquire a "brainbox." But there are also shopping trips (outfit yourself with cyberlegs) and small vignettes (pick up Lou at home, stepping over her snoring boyfriend). Your only real opponent is the environment. How to climb that wall? How to jump to a far-off train? How to get inside? How to get downstairs? How to get through a tight space you can't get through? Where is the package? How to launch yourself back if you left your launcher?

Chung has developed his universe considerably in *Quadrilateral Cowboy*. Above all, it's more systemically complex, and more based in a traditional progression of problem-solving and mechanics. It's a much longer game, with more levels, and the detail seems to go on forever. If you take the time to look closely, paintings on the walls have plaques with the artist's name and the piece's title; the bookshelves are stacked with absurd titles that never were. There are also references to earlier games, a continuing geography—the clocks on the airship in the Malta Stock Exchange level show the local times for "Vire River," "Zauberberg," and "West Egg," each of which first appeared on the big board at Cugat Airfield in *Thirty Flights of Loving*.

Another strategy Chung employs is diegesis—that is, the effects within the game all take place within the game. You don't press a button and zip out of the game for a moment to study the manual—the manual is an actual thing you carry in the game and can look at while still within *Quadrilateral Cowboy*. If it's dark where you are, you have to turn on a lantern to see it. There is no soundtrack—there is only the music of your portable Vinylman and various turntables you come across, which you can switch on or off as you prefer. This is a nice touch, certainly, and part of the feeling of really being in this world, not half-in and half-on your couch. Nothing in the game happens outside the world you're in, no swelling orchestra from above to tell you to feel sad or angry or happy, no jumping out of the universe to check your stats. And in what seems like another nice touch, when you walk into a chair, you hear yourself, as Poncho, let out a muffled grunt. And then discover the chair's in your way. You can push it forward, or walk around it, or jump over it, but when you walk into things, you bump into them. Later, this will turn out to be useful, not just a detail. The game surprises you this way, as you categorize this over here as a useless ornament, and that over there as useful information, and then discover your categories don't match the universe you're in quite as neatly as you thought. If games are in any way practice for life outside the circle, that's as good a lesson as any.

7

THE THEME OF THE TRAITOR AND THE HERO

But maybe games don't have to be practice at all. Maybe they don't have to be fun. If games can provide higher meaning, can they be art? Art doesn't have to be fun. It can offer other things. The divide between AAA games, the big multimillion-dollar blockbusters, and indie games, made by solo practitioners or smaller teams, could begin just as a question of quantities of money and labor, but in truth when you have a single mind responsible for making something and a group of minds responsible for making something, there are bound to be differences, and differences that head in strange directions. Even the blockbusters can do things you might call art—new, innovative approaches to creating a thing that leads an audience to feel and learn and know things they didn't before.

Shigeru Miyamoto, beginning at Nintendo, hoped that

video games might spring from the Bible and Shakespeare as much as Tolkien and Star Trek, and now they have, to some degree. What began as a technological experiment and transformed itself into a massive business has also found there is room for games that spring from somebody's strange dreams, a corner for games for games' sake. It has found room for political, sociological, historical, or cultural artifacts—a game about the 1979 Iranian Revolution, say, or a game about cancer and the death of a child. Some innovators are just interested in doing things the way they want to do things; others set out to deliberately do things differently, even to join an aesthetic tradition outside the history of games. There is an ever-growing game auteur tradition, and there are game designers who want to vex the question of what a game can be, and game designers who make things that have more in common with video installations you might see at an art gallery than they do with *Donkey Kong*, and there are game designers who intend to create gaming's *Citizen Kane*, designers who think it is time for the medium to produce the games that will match the *Iliad* and *Guernica* and *Kind of Blue*. Then there are also the other game designers who think those game designers are stupid.

For Chung, these categories don't apply. He makes

games. He likes people to be able to play them. He doesn't make the games everyone else is making. He makes things that didn't exist before. He makes the dreams in his head. But he also develops those dreams by thinking very carefully about what those dreams might do for the people playing. He started *Quadrilateral Cowboy*, as he usually starts his games, with an idea and a set of limitations, and moved on to making a test prototype level. "So that was the level that I brought to all the expos and shows, and thus it got a lot of iteration from just players playing it and banging on it and breaking it in different ways," he told me. "It just gets touched so much that it gets a lot of love."

"At the beginning of a project, at the very least for me, the game is kind of a very amorphous blob: it doesn't know what it wants to be. And I don't know what it wants to be," he said. He'd originally planned an ambitious scope, to create a giant world; then thought of a really detailed simulation of a city block; and finally landed on making modular chunks, more like "a traditional video game," he said. Among the things he did that were less traditional, though, was to build it in public. What Chung did was livestream his work. Since 2013, once or twice a week, Chung has displayed what was happening on his screen, narrating it and working on it as you watched. He'll say things like, "Today, we're fixing the right-click thingy here, because people aren't seeing it," or, "I'm wondering if this could be a particle effect instead," and then explain how he was fixing it as you watched him fiddle with the script.

People who are watching Chung work discuss it on-screen in chats. Sometimes he answers their questions. Sometimes they make suggestions. "Wasn't it printing velocity when the bullets actually fired?" one writes, as Chung struggles with something. "Could be wrong, but it seemed like it was working." Chung reads it. "Oh my god, you're right!" he says. "It was working the whole time!" Not only does he provide a look into the creation of the game, he offers his mistakes, his wrong turns, his ruts. He's just made an animation for Maisy, on the boat: she does pull-ups. Now he's trying to make Lou sit on a box. "Uh-oh. Why . . . is she doing that? Hm. Ohh. Okay. So this is the origin point, by her feet. Eh. Looks okay. But the next time I make this model I should probably also detach the head from the body. With the legs, I can move them wherever I want, because they're detached from the armature, but the head—I made the mistake of clamping it on.

"So I have an idea . . . let's see if this works or not. I'm kinda curious how it would look if I added a specular map to her glasses." He changes Maisy's glasses. "A specular map determines—it's basically how shiny something is. How it catches the light. Let's see how it looks." He works on it. "Whoa. That looks weird. I think this might not actually work at all . . . Nope. Let's scrap that. Doesn't look right to me. The good part about source control is that you can basically press undo on a ton of changes. Brrmp!"

And once the game has shipped, this doesn't change. "People are definitely finding ways to break the game in lots of ways," he told me. "One I thought was pretty fun was that in the game, you can pick up a chair and throw it out a window, do whatever you want with it, and people figured out that if they stood on top of a chair, and then tried to pick it up, the chair would levitate into the sky. The player just rises up, like a floating cloud. The player just enters heaven, I guess."

Which is where the gods are. Whether those gods are making addictive widgets, or sophisticated entertainments, or art objects—that is a category question, and endlessly debatable. But why shouldn't they be able to make all three? There are famous authorial figures in the game world, from Miyamoto on down, great geniuses who transformed what games did and do, creators of great works of brilliance, who blessed a grateful audience with their creations. And some of them exert more control over what their games can do than others. But if video games can be presented as art, they will be a different kind of art. Every age finds its own responses to its present. Drama and poetry became insufficient, so we invented the novel; painting and sculpture became insufficient, and so we invented the photograph, and when that wasn't enough, film and television. The path to creation, for video games, again, takes place in a consensual relationship between designer and player. This art object is not consumed, but instead given life, once it is finished. The two sides of its coin, its creator and its consumer, trade places. The hero creates; the traitor makes a choice. Together they make something new.

Chung admires many designers, loves all sorts of games, but he doesn't particularly think of game design as a grand authorial gift from on high. Not only is he interested in including players in the creation of a thing, but he doesn't think the ability to make games requires genius or an extraordinary set of skills. What he describes is similar to researcher Carol Dweck's concept of growth mindset—the concept that talents and abilities can be developed and that challenges set that development. "A lot of times, I'm saying, 'I don't know how to do this,'" Chung told me, speaking about the livestreams.

"It's not about knowing everything—it's about being willing to say, 'I'll just figure out how to do it right now.' It's about being able to teach yourself how to find information."

That's the way it seems Tom Cadwell has hired his teams, looking for people who are good at learning, rather than people who already learned it all. That said, for *League of Legends*, designing for inclusion and freedom are a bit different, in part because the game is a game of mastery, and giving people a consistent experience of climbing a continuing hill of mastery can't be as loose with its sense of control. And because it's a multiplayer game, unlike Chung's games, allowing a player to do just about whatever he or she wants has effects on everybody else's experience. If you give a hundred million players more of a free hand in how your game unspools, you might get one monkey with a typewriter who taps out *King Lear*, but also ninety-nine million people who stopped playing your game. And finally, when you have the livelihood of thousands of employees and billions of dollars at stake, there's a little less room for a "let's see what the player makes of it" attitude. Still, this is hardly to say that *Quadrilateral Cowboy* is formless, nor that *League of Legends* players are passive receptors. They both have rules to their universes. You can't blow off your friends Maisy and Lou;

you can't kill your teammates in Summoner's Rift. "Games have a collection of design pillars and frameworks that you abide by," Cadwell said. "I mean, in *God of War*, for instance, there's a bible of things that the protagonists will or won't do." (*God of War* is a third-person combat-puzzle game in which you play Kratos, a Spartan warrior adrift in a dangerous world.) "The main guy, he's a super-competent character, he actually never steps backward, he only moves forward. So if you tell him to go backward, he turns around and goes in that direction, and actually never takes backward steps. He's too confident of a warrior to do that. He never retreats."

Though there may be unbreakable rules, the *LoL* community is nothing if not engaged; the Riot teams dedicated to following what players are saying about the game and asking of it are vital to design decisions and drive a lot of choices. And Cadwell is an admirer of the invention some *LoL* players display in their attempts to outgame the game. "Our players found this bug where they basically bottleneck all minions spawning from their nexus," he told me. "They would just bottleneck them up, and then they removed the turrets, and then the minions just come out in this unstoppable wave, a thousand minions who could not be destroyed." He thought that one was clever. Sometimes there are just mistakes—

Riot once mistakenly shipped a champion who couldn't be killed. The players found that one quick. "There's certainly some choices you make as a designer where you just make it easier over time to ensure that people can get there if they keep trying," Cadwell said. "But then there's also situations where players will play the game in ways you're not expecting: they've decided their goals are not the goals you had in mind. They're losing by your definition, but they've formed a different goal and they're feeling satisfaction about that. So we do have problems in game design, for sure, when the player has adopted a goal that the mechanisms of the game, the mechanics of the game system, don't really support." But they also learn about the things their game can do that they hadn't planned. Those sorts of alternate goals may mess with what everyone else is doing—if you're just wandering around Summoner's Rift, looking at the pretty landscape and not fighting, your team is going to lose and your team is also going to be annoyed. But all the same: you can choose.

And for the other part, Chung is hardly making esoteric dreams for his own entertainment: he has won a shelfful of prizes and awards (among them, the Independent Games Festival Grand Prize and the IGF Excellence in Design award) and sold more than a million copies of his games. At an average of about ten dollars a game, that's plenty to keep him in business, but it also represents a great number of people who have committed their money to the prospect that a Blendo game will give them something they haven't had before.

This is all to say, any design style—loose hold or tight grip—ultimately can't stop the art object, or consumer product, whatever a video game is, from coming into full existence only once it has players banging on it, and exactly what kind of banging is still mostly up to them. Take sports: nobody ever called basketball, or soccer, an art form, but what Michael Jordan or Pelé did with the game has been compared to the beauty and truth of poetry. The realization of the structure in living motion changes it. Games in this sense are living texts, unfinished and dynamic, stories filled with blank pages for the reader to write. In that regard, you can't possibly say, for instance, that Chung is making art and Cadwell entertainment. The difference doesn't exist in the way it used to. This is a new kind of collaborative aesthetic—artist and consumer are no longer such clear and viable categories. Because what the person using the object, transforming the object, has to say about what it is has as much to do with what it is and what it does as does the person who began the creation of the object in the first place.

8

METAPHORS WERE A WEARINESS OF THE FLESH TO THE POETS THEMSELVES

In a half century or so, games have moved from two dimensions, a few fuzzy lines and a dot on a screen, to planes of virtual reality. The technology has caught up with the mind's magic circle: VR and AR will place you inside alternative dimensions of the universe, blanket a physical space with an overlay all around you. Whatever's next, in part, will be probed and tested by game designers. When philosophers suggest that it's possible, considering the exponential progress of computer technology, that we are living in nothing more than a computer simulation of life, just a universe created by some programmer who created a world to see what it would be like to put a bunch of bipeds on a blue planet and let them knock around for a few million years of simulated existence, they could just be talking about an advanced game that someone's playing, all of human history nothing more than a single afternoon on a couch for some kid in the thirtieth century.

Maybe, maybe not. But it's certainly an argument worth considering that in the twenty-first century designing and playing games represent something different from the pursuits they're usually compared to. Eric Zimmerman thinks games can change culture more dramatically than other arts and entertainments. In his "Manifesto for a Ludic Century," he writes: "In the Ludic Century, we cannot have a passive relationship to the systems that we inhabit. We must learn to be designers, to recognize how and why systems are constructed, and to try to make them better." Games, he says, "alter the very nature of cultural consumption. Music is *played* by musicians, but most people are not musicians—they listen to music that someone else has made. Games, on the other hand, require active participation. Game design involves systems logic, social psychology, and culture hacking. To play a game deeply is to think more and more like a game designer—to tinker, retro-engineer, and modify a game in order to find new ways to play. As more people play more deeply in the Ludic Century, the lines will become increasingly blurred between game players and game designers."

So if you're going to design video games, be prepared: you may be responsible for transforming the culture. You may be responsible for systemic change. One helpful example of the way games can have a different role in and influence on the culture from other forms of art and entertainment—and of the way game developers have to think differently about the ethics of their creation—was provided to me by Ananda Gupta, who is principal game designer at Riot. Gupta told me, "Because games ask you to take action and to make decisions in ways that books and movies don't, that changes how we can treat controversial topics." For instance, he said, "Nobody would bat an eye at reading Albert Speer's book about how he structured the Nazi economy. Even though it's written by him in the first person. And yet playing a game where you are Albert Speer organizing the Nazi economy feels very, very different from that." Something very different is happening cognitively between those two experiences. For some players, it might just be unpleasant to have the Nazis' goals be their goals in a game. Some might like it. Others might ignore the ethical questions. But whichever way, the participatory nature of that experience has a different effect on the brain. It would be a very different thing to read a memoir about genocide from attempting to win at a simulation of it. In the book, you look into a murderer's mind. In the game, you become him. There can be little doubt that these are not the same.

The unreality of the magic circle always has a relation to the reality outside it.

"I feel deeply that we can't avoid the responsibility to better understand the impact of the products that we're creating," Kimberly Voll, who worked at Riot as a principal technical director and head of player dynamics, and has now co-founded her own game company, told me. Voll studied cognitive science in college and did a PhD in computer science, with a focus on AI, and taught at the University of British Columbia for six years before entering the game industry full-time. "I think as a society we need to understand these mechanisms much better than we presently do," she said. "In a sense, I don't think it's too dramatic to say that intelligence is fast becoming the last commodity. Right? It is the last thing we will trade over, and somebody will win. And that will have deep, deep consequences for how we are structured as a society, for how we are capable of or even allowed to relate to one another. We're ceding control over a lot more than I think most people realize. This sounds very alarmist and I don't intend it that way. But we need to ask the right questions about how information is filtered before it reaches us, as different filtration systems replace the old ones."

Are games really going to be that important in choosing what information our society uses? If they can be art objects, they can also be cultural artifacts, records of what we were and are and hope to be. They can be ethical and moral objects. They can affect how we learn. They can be games about pattern-recognition and they can be games about history. They can be about the War of 1812 and they can be about climate change conflict and they can be about the moral choices our future selves will face as we evolve into transhumanism, when we are no longer human. They can affect what information goes where. Much of this is probably up for debate, and we'll see, I suppose, over time. But for everyone who thinks video games are some distasteful fringe sector of the culture, there are some billions who would disagree, who are living and dying in their games—spending and earning not just money, but spending and earning more social and cultural capital there than nongamers could imagine, learning and thinking and growing in response to the games and the communities that have grown within them—as a counterpoint. Bleeding-edge technology tends to go where the money is, and a very large amount of the money now is certainly sitting in games. If it is possible that the twenty-first century will only see an increase in how much time we spend online, how much substance of ourselves we put online, games will have a role in that. We've played since we were human, and long before. As technology is inserted into more and more corners of human life— and as play increasingly simulates, reflects, distorts, and corrects more and more corners of human life—it would be foolish to reject the idea that thinking about what goes into making these games is useful, that it matters what they're telling us, what they're teaching us, what they're telling us about ourselves.

So does this affect how designers make their games? "I work a lot via design pillars," Voll said. "I want to understand: What are our lighthouses? What are the things that we look up to, that we rely on as focusing mechanisms? Sometimes those will change over time. And so when it comes down to, do I add this gun that fires bubbles or that gun that, I don't know, high-fives your opponent, you're always asking how does that ladder up to those pillars? And so for us, you know, one of those pillars is cooperative play." Co-op games, like the one Voll and her colleagues at their new company are making, are an increasingly popular genre—they require players to work together as teammates, usually not against other people but against AIs. The current pinnacle of this cooperative creation, perhaps, is a game called *Dreams* (2020), in which there are no quests, or kills, or puzzles, except of your own making. *Dreams* is a game in which the player creates a game. It requires no code. Hundreds and thousands of games are taking shape in *Dreams*, some by individual players, others by teams, others by strangers contributing bits of a whole, players remixing and remaking other players' work. Games are based in contests, but those contests don't have to pit human beings against each other—they can teach us how to work together better. "We think now is the time to change the culture of game development," Voll said, when she announced her new company, Stray Bombay. "We want to build games that reflect our culture."

Voll is thinking about how games affect the way people relate to each other, but she's not at a think tank: she's starting a company. She wants to create games that people will enjoy and purchase, while at the same time asking the right questions along the way. At the same time, there is a rapidly growing industry of explicitly educational games,

games designed for children with special needs, games for Alzheimer's patients, games to teach you coding, and games to teach you economics. Nonprofits like Games for Change, founded in 2004, have staked out the mission of helping game creators work toward the social good, "using games and technology that help people to learn, improve their communities, and contribute to make the world a better place."

In 2016, Voll co-created a project outside of Riot, a game called *Fantastic Contraption*. It's a puzzle game in virtual reality: players use the motion controls and a VR headset to construct machines of their own devising. While some designers think games are games, and new technology doesn't change the foundations, Voll does think that VR represents a new horizon. VR is essentially nonlinear, and it's incredibly hard for a designer to exercise any kind of control over the player. And you are there—you are inside—in an absolutely new way. "We're establishing the language of VR, we're establishing the rules of VR," she told a Game Developers Conference crowd in 2016. Those rules will be important when you think about the extent to which the universe we inhabit increasingly seems to be overtaken and replaced by a metaverse—a virtual existence, where society and economics and love and death take place in another reality. And where have we seen the beginnings of that? In *World of Warcraft*. In *Fortnite*. In games. Those rules will be important when you think about how much of reality we've replaced with metaphors for reality—stand-ins, simulations, new identities, new sensations. Distinguishing the two won't always be so easy. At some point, the distinction will begin to disappear.

9

MANIFESTATIONS OF IMAGINATION

In October 2019, *League of Legends* turned ten, and Riot Games, long referred to in jest as "Riot Game," since *League of Legends* was its only game, added the plural in earnest. In addition to all manner of celebration of their flagship property, Riot announced eight new games in production, including a first-person shooter ("Project A"), a *League of Legends* fighting game ("Project L"), an open-world game ("Project F"), and a digital card game (*Legends of Runeterra*). All the new games, with the exception of the shooter, take place in the world of Runeterra.

The new games all fell under the umbrella of Cadwell's position as head of R&D, though by this point in his career he was doing considerably less of any kind of day-to-day design decision-making than he once did. There was, after all, an empire to oversee. *Fortnite* may have taken *League of Legends'* top spot in gaming, but Riot—which by then had made

$20 billion since its founding—had been holding a few tricks up its sleeve. The new games produced their own degree of hysteria in the gamer world, but Riot also indicated a new direction: horizontal expansion, you might call it. Not only were they introducing new games, and not only were they expanding to mobile gaming, but they were also introducing a series of books, comics, an animated television show, and a partnership with the fashion brand Louis Vuitton (including champion skins and a "Summoner's Cup Trunk" for the *LoL* championship trophy). The company also introduced Riot Forge, a publishing label within Riot Games intended to complement Riot's R&D wing, contracting working studios outside of Riot Games to create "bespoke 'completable' *League of Legends* games," created and developed by their partner studios and published by Riot Forge.

As this was going on, Cadwell was busier and busier, but still found perhaps his greatest pleasure in design. He saw his career comprised of three or four parts. First, the practice of direct design, often smaller parts of a whole. The next stage had been product leadership, directing teams. Third, more strategic thinking, as in, "Where should we be innovating? What should those innovations look like? How big or small should we go, which problems should we prioritize?" One of the great things he'd learned over the years, as he entered into new leadership roles—and now, looking at the increasingly bigger picture, coaching and training designers, managing the R&D pipeline, overseeing new projects, and evaluating proposed ones—was how much of the art of design had to do with choosing not to do things. "The choices you make to *not* do something are at the core of it," he said, "because there's so much you can do, so much you could do, and really for any game that's innovative, it turns out there's a handful of things that matter and there's a ton of stuff that doesn't." Distinguishing the two, he felt, had really turned out to be the trick.

This big-picture stuff didn't mean Cadwell had given up doing actual design and moved entirely into management. The problems of how to make a game work the best way it can still got him animated. "Take *Legends of Runeterra*," he said of the digital card game. "One example of what the team had to figure out was: What percent of the time when you make an action should that action be interfered with by your opponent? So. Right. That's one where if the answer is never, your action is never interfered with, the game doesn't have what they call interactive strategy. If I play my game and you play your game there's a winner, but there's no interaction, and it's not a strategy game. But then of course, if most of my actions are getting messed with by you, then the game becomes entirely about what's in your head, what's in your hand, and not about what am I doing. And that feels also unsatisfying, and the tolerance for that really depends upon the experience of all players."

About a year before, Blendo Games had released a trailer for *Skin Deep*, Brendon Chung's new game in development. *Skin Deep* is a new experience for Chung, an immersive sim, set in space. You're an insurance company security contractor prowling a cargo starship with a head cold and no shoes, on the lookout for pirates. This time you can actually shoot, wandering around the spaceship, protecting your employers' cargo. The music is Edvard Grieg, *Peer Gynt*; the premise is a deadshot commando who can't stop sneezing. You could watch Chung's progress twice a week.

Meanwhile, I'd been playing a few other, mostly metafictional—or meta-ludic—games, games meant to mess around with some of what games are meant to be. In *The Stanley Parable* (2011), a walking-puzzle game, the indie developer Davey Wreden plays with allowing a player to ignore the game's rules, and in his *The Beginner's Guide* (2015), he plays with notions of authorship and the spaces between virtual or projected identities and real ones. In *Papers, Please* (2013), another indie game, you play the role of a border agent in a fictional Central European country, having to make ethical choices about whether to follow the increasingly complex rules about who may enter the country. And in *The Magic Circle* (2015), you are a quality assurance tester on a game that is half-finished, stuck in development for almost two decades after the massive success of its prequel, with the developers arguing as you proceed about whether to let you kill anyone and whether the forest is too confusing and so on.

The Magic Circle is a puzzle-adventure open-world game set in a magical universe, split between spaceships and magical forests, with strange creatures and magic mushroom wizards; you gain power over these characters by trapping them and then hacking their motivations and behaviors— make an enemy into an ally, then swapping around powers so the ally can be more useful—until eventually you figure out things like: to get up to a high place or across a river of lava, for instance, you need to give the flying power of a whirligig to a juggodillo, which you can stand on, and then ride up in the air. The game requires creative problem-solving, ignoring the paths the overcontrolling designers have set out for you—you are not a mortal walking a world made by a god; you are a god yourself. Finally, you break out of the game—and are asked to finish designing the game yourself. I designed one.

Mine was awful.

I'd asked Cadwell for a thought experiment: say I was rich, and bored, and loved video games, and decided to make one, and wanted to hire him to consult on the design of my game. Did it matter that I knew nothing? Nothing about the reams of research regarding the effects of different lights and colors on the brain? Nothing about the way the different channels of the brain process different kinds of information? Not much idea about the differences between *Overwatch* and *Fortnite* and *Apex Legends*? Well sure, he said, Riot has designers with PhDs in cognitive neuroscience, in computer science, in group psychology, and so on. They have people thinking about these things very deeply. There's a lot of knowledge. Moreover, Riot hires people who play games all the time and have thought about the differences between *Overwatch* and *Fortnite* and *Apex Legends* quite a bit on their own. But he also pointed out that when I'd asked him about fundamental principles that had meant something to him early on in his career, he'd answered yes, very early in learning about these things, he'd been struck by the idea of the flow state, and more generally, the idea that one ideal cycle for a game would go from arousal to stress to relaxation, and then repeat. "But this is also reflected in the three-act play," Cadwell said, "and did they have cognitive neuroscience in ancient Greece?" For all the scientific analysis of gameplay, human intuition about what's interesting and meaningful often has as much value as all the research in the world.

I proposed a sort of mythological battle royale game. Norse gods against Greek gods (Thor versus Ares!) and Aztec gods versus Slavic gods (Quetzalcóatl against Chernobog!) and so on. The old question: Who would win in a fight, Batman or Superman? Also, I wanted nine-year-olds to be able to play it together. Cadwell looked slightly dubious, but said, "Well, you *could* make a good game out of what you're describing." The first thing to do, he said, was to clearly establish your goals, and then to play with the constraints of the game and explore other games. And investigate the parts of the system. "What are the pieces that are interesting to you? And why are they interesting to you?

"A lot of games could support playing together and mythology. What I would do is look at what are the types of co-op games that nine-year-olds can play at all," he said.

"And so first you're going to play a couple of different genres until you have some understanding of the genres. We're not talking months of research here—you can figure this out pretty quick through online searches. You could ask your kids' friends, what are they playing that's resonating with them. And then you would play the best examples of these games. Some will be player versus player, some will be player versus environment. Some are going to be some combination. I would say for that age range, you typically see fewer PVP games and more co-op versus environment games. You'll also play some side-in games that you think are compelling."

"What's 'side-in'?" I asked.

"'Side-in' says, if I take this game and change it twenty percent, then I'll have the thing I'm looking for. That's how most game development is done. If you do something more dramatically, dramatically innovative, if you go back to the basic drawing board of genres, that's a much longer, harder process. If you say, I like some aspects of this genre and some of that genre, but what I really want to do is create some new genre—well, that's a much more difficult task. But in the case of this game, I would say you play a wide variety of genres that could fit. And that forces you to make choices about which of your goals are the best. And then you circle back from your initial pitch, which was rough-shod, and say, 'I've learned all this stuff. I thought what I wanted was, *Mythology Street Fighter*, or *Soulcalibur for Nine-Year-Olds*, but now I've realized what I really wanted was, you know, say, *Mythology Double Dragon* or *Mythology Castle Crashers*.' And that narrowing of the innovation window allows you to say, okay, fine, I'm holding a bunch of this stuff within this genre constant, so then what further things do I need to make this game successful and where might I innovate? The more you can guide the team and yourself as a designer to answer the question—this is important to innovate, and that isn't—the better. There are times when innovation isn't solving a problem and may just cause problems down the line. You don't innovate everything. You innovate where it's going to achieve your goals."

As Cadwell began gearing up, showing me games that were strong on one aspect of the game I was proposing—this one was designed well to demand a substantively cooperative approach but didn't tell a story well, and then that one did the opposite, another introduced a riddling puzzle aspect that appealed to me but was maybe too much for nine-year-olds—he began putting together pieces, trying them in different fits together, constructing a system out of a puzzle whose pieces had not been designed to go together ever before.

"If you're saying you want the players to experience being a god as a protagonist, then presumably you want to make them feel godlike," he was saying.

"Right," I said.

"And if they're fighting peer-level gods, they're not going to feel very godlike, because peer-level gods would just be like human fighting human. Even if you're mixing up mythologies and, you know, I'm Athena, and I'm battling it out with, say, Thor or something, you should expect we're pretty evenly matched." He was really moving now. "Of course you could try, for instance, tons and tons of supernatural creatures and cultists and whatever that don't really pose a large threat to you but in large numbers can be a distraction to you. But then there's also a question, even for a game like that, does it even make sense that a mortal could wound Athena? It kind of doesn't. Maybe a supernatural creature could, but you might consider whether you should make your player characters demigods, supported by the gods. Or maybe you have to fight them, if you're Hercules, eventually you have to fight Hades, as an end boss, and to fight the god of death, well, there's a scale there, too. He should be stronger than me. But it shouldn't be that he is guaranteed in all circumstances to defeat me. He should just have a ninety-nine point nine percent lock on it . . ."

In just a few minutes, Cadwell had taken me through a dramatically deeper understanding of the game I wanted to make, what its implications and parameters were and weren't, the ways it could work, the ways it couldn't. It was a structure by structure, detail by detail sort of process. There were no universe-creating gods here, at that moment, no grand divine sweep of creation, only thinkers, builders, constructors of stories and structures, block by block. "Mechanics and systems are the nouns and the verbs that we're using to create an experience," he said.

And finally—what was the value of those experiences? What was a designer designing? Some of it, Cadwell thought, might be just substitutions for other experiences—instead of the coffee shop, or the bowling league, community is increasingly formed online, and particularly in games. "Culture broadly provides meaning for people where they need meaning," he said, "and in Western nations in particular, persistent communities over recent years have been eroded. Community in general is harder to find. And I personally think humans are happier, and stronger, when they're members of strong communities. And I think that games are able to do a lot more to contribute to community than some of the other technological creations of the age." And beyond that? What would games do? Some of it is the work of mapping a human culture, the creation of something that, until now, has never been: Brendon Chung making something new that had not existed before, but is also made up of the blocks of culture that had come from the past, swirled and mixed and in conversation, until that mix realized itself into something entirely new. What else? They would continue to allow us to play a new thing. The road of play continuing. Imitating and defining the present, mapping the possible futures. Creating systems to cut out corners of the universe and name them.

Back to bits and pieces cobbled together. All these constraints! What about creating a universe? When would designing games become that utter freedom that playing games was supposed to be? The untrammeled power of divine creation? Much of the future of games has to do with technology—an unlimited vista, created by new tools we will invent to bend reality to our will. Perhaps we will enter a metaverse, an unlimited collective cyberspace, and then never leave it, having uploaded our consciousnesses to a great game in the cloud, unconstrained by bodies, unbound by the earth. But art and innovation have always sprung from constraints—and been constraints in and of themselves. They are structures imposed on an unstructured reality. The placing of form upon formlessness, or upon forms we cannot see without naming them, cannot understand without giving them color and sound and language. The imposition of meaning on life. The three-act play, yes, as well as the infinite depictions of the Buddha, the paintings upon paintings of Jesus washing the feet of the lepers: all constraints on what you can paint, what you can see, but allowing for limitless variation. Until that variation leaves its constraint. If the magic circle is an unreal space, it is also in some sense a holy space: a place of faith. Faith in something that lies beyond it. What game are we playing when the shadows cast on the cave replace the cave itself? When the manifestations of an imagination begin to appear in real life? When the metaverse, that fictional place, becomes real and swallows the universe it was created within? When the systems defining an unreal world escape, and cast a net over the real one, and become it themselves.

FURTHER READING

A few good places to start: *Rules of Play*, by Eric Zimmerman and Katie Salen, is excellent and goes through both some nuts and bolts as well more theoretical perspectives on what a designer is actually trying to achieve and how that happens. *The Art of Game Design: A Book of Lenses*, by the game designer Jesse Schell, is similarly useful. Tracy Fullerton's *Game Design Workshop* is also valuable.

Chris Crawford's *The Art of Computer Game Design*, which came out in 1984, was the first book of the video game age to try to describe what a video game designer does. His later book, *Chris Crawford on Game Design* (2003) is also good. For more on what underlies all this, Raph Koster's work provides another view—*A Theory of Fun for Game Design* is in fact a lot of fun. For history and context, there's *Blood, Sweat, and Pixels* (2017), by Jason Schreier; *Console Wars* (2015), by Blake J. Harris; *A History of Video Games in 64 Objects*, by the Strong's World Video Game

Hall of Fame; *Smartbomb: The Quest for Art, Entertainment, and Big Bucks in the Videogame Revolution*, by Heather Chaplin and Aaron Ruby; and *Handmade Pixels: Independent Video Games and the Quest for Authenticity*, by Jesper Juul.

For a more theoretical discussion of play, study starts with Johan Huizinga's *Homo Ludens* and moves on to the French sociologist Roger Caillois: *Man, Play and Games.* I also liked Juul's books *Half-Real: Video Games between Real Rules and Fictional Worlds* and *The Art of Failure: An Essay on the Pain of Playing Video Games*, and Tom Bissell's *Extra Lives: Why Video Games Matter.*

On the internet, the world of game design is open to you—a thousand videos and blogs dedicated to how to design a game. Many game designers and game theorists have their own sites. For a wider view, there's also gamasutra.com and kotaku.com, and the newsletter from Jamin Warren's game consultancy, Twofivesix, (https://twofivesix.co/newsletter) is wonderfully smart.

ACKNOWLEDGMENTS

Thanks to Tom Cadwell and Brendon Chung.

Thanks to Alex Abramovich.

Thanks to Laeti Lorétan, Jordan Schmidt, Nabil Kassem, Naomi McArthur, Christina Norman, Stone Librande, Dan Emmons, John Frank, Ananda Gupta, Andrei Van Roon, Buiko Ndefo-Dahl, Reina Sweet, and Kimberly Voll. Thanks to Eric Zimmerman. Thanks to Jon-Paul Dyson and Jeremy Saucier. Thanks to Machi Davis. Thanks to Dave Setiadi. Thanks to Jamin Warren. Thanks to Cliff Sahlin and to Jane Larsen and to Pierre Menard. Thanks to Christina Shay.

Thanks to Stuart Roberts and to Emily Simonson and to Cary Goldstein.

Thanks to Calvin and Sasha and Macy; thanks to Joe and Joan.

Thanks, above all, to Christina Lewis.

ABOUT THE AUTHOR

Daniel Noah Halpern has written stories and essays for magazines including the *New Yorker*, the *New York Times Magazine*, *GQ*, and *Harper's*. He lives in New York City with his family.